BEL CANTO

Bel Canto

The Teaching of the Classical Italian Song-Schools, its Decline and Restoration

LUCIE MANÉN

Oxford   New York

OXFORD UNIVERSITY PRESS

OXFORD
UNIVERSITY PRESS

Great Clarendon Street, Oxford OX2 6DP

Oxford University Press is a department of the University of Oxford.
It furthers the University's objective of excellence in research, scholarship,
and education by publishing worldwide in

Oxford New York

Auckland Bangkok Buenos Aires Cape Town Chennai
Dar es Salaam Delhi Hong Kong Istanbul Karachi Kolkata
Kuala Lumpur Madrid Melbourne Mexico City Mumbai Nairobi
São Paulo Shanghai Taipei Tokyo Toronto

Oxford is a registered trade mark of Oxford University Press
in the UK and in certain other countries

Published in the United States
by Oxford University Press Inc., New York

British Library Cataloguing in Publication Data

Manén, Lucie
Bel canto: the teaching of the classical
Italian song-schools: its decline and
restoration.
1. Bel Canto
I. Title II. Manén, Lucie. Art of singing
784.9'4 MT845

Library of Congress Cataloging in Publication Data
Manén, Lucie.
Bel canto.
Rev. ed. of: The art of singing. 1974
Bibliography: p. 73.
1. Singing—Instruction and study. I. Manén, Lucie.
Art of singing. II. Title.
MT820.M26 1987 784.9'32 87-11245
ISBN 0-19-317109-0

5 7 9 10 8 6

Printed in Great Britain on acid-free paper by
Biddles Short-Run Books
King's Lynn

PREFACE

by Professor Brian Trowell

I have been concerned all my life with the history and practice of opera, particularly early opera, and have been fascinated by singers, singing, the art of vocal interpretation, and the craft of coaching. For some twenty five years I have observed the development of Lucie Manén's research on voice-production. I have experienced her teaching in her studio, and at times coached her pupils. I have advised her on matters relating to the history and theory of music and assisted, in a small way, with the preparation of her earlier book, *The Art of Singing* (London: Faber Music Ltd., 1974). I have helped to arrange and have introduced lectures and lecture-demonstrations by Lucie Manén at the University of London, where she first propounded in public her ideas and method of teaching, here gathered into such a persuasive sequence of argument and exposition. I feel very honoured by the invitation to introduce her book to a much wider public; it offers them, in definitive form, the findings of her admirable scientific research, guided always by her extraordinary gifts of intuition and musical understanding, and achieved through single-minded self-discipline and long years of hard application.

This book is a lifetime's work. It was completed in the teeth of many extraordinary twists and turns in her personal and professional life, which she managed to overcome with her formidable energy. Such an authoritative and stimulating exposition of the decline and restoration of the lost Bel Canto tradition is of historical importance in its own right; but its immortality is also guaranteed by its practical importance as a touchstone for future generations of musicians, singers, and singing teachers.

I first became aware of Lucie Manén by listening to two broadcast talks on the BBC Third Programme. One was about the five soprano roles in *The Marriage of Figaro*, the other a comparison of various interpretations of Gilda's 'Caro nome' in *Rigoletto*. I had never heard such a remarkable blend of interpretative insights brought to bear with such transforming effect on music which I had thought I knew well. What was so extraordinary was not so much her command of historical and analytical issues, or her sense of character and dramatic situation; it was the way in which she spoke with such authority and such luminous understanding of the means by which the application of different vocal colours and different kinds of phrasing and articulation are to be placed at the service of music. These two talks quite changed my comprehension of the art of opera. I was not surprised, therefore, to discover that Lucie Manén was also a remarkable teacher, to whom such eminent singers as Elizabeth Harwood and Sir Peter Pears turned for expert advice.

Lucie Manén's *Bel Canto* is a textbook different from most others known to me, in that it is based on the newest findings of scientific research, conducted with modern methods and equipment; it reposes on the advice and co-operation of an array of eminent scientists who are named in the annotations.

Very few singing teachers have received scientific training, and there is the danger that some may react with surprise, reservation, annoyance, or downright antagonism, rather than feel stimulated or creatively challenged by the advent of Lucie Manén's new and unfamiliar theories. But they ought not to avoid asking themselves the question 'What, in fact, is my teaching based on?' The most successful career — however valuable the experience may be in some respects — does not qualify a singer to set up as a teacher. Ambitious pupils always feel attracted by the big names. Yet it is only a few advanced pupils who mature to perfection in so-called master-classes. What ought to matter most is the basic instruction of a pupil at the introductory and intermediate stages: this requires individual tuition by a teacher who — apart from having been a singer—possesses at least some up-to-date and accurate basic knowledge in anatomy, physiology, musical acoustics, and psychology. Without this, what teacher can honestly claim to be competent, or presume to show a pupil how to build his or her instrument for singing—an instrument which consists of a great deal more than just the larynx—and how to 'play' that instrument?

'The need for interdisciplinary training for singing teachers' was a theme propounded by Lucie Manén as early as 1974 at the Eleventh International Conference of the International Society for Musical Education, held at the University of Perth in Western Australia. I have attempted since about that time to convince various institutions of the need to set up proper courses for the interdisciplinary training of singing teachers: so far, in vain. Some of those whom I approached seemed content that the tutors for whom they were responsible should continue their teaching with no valid basis in psychophysiological theory; others feared a negative response to such new ideas, stimulating and creatively challenging though they might be.

The publication of this book must surely herald a change of attitude. Lucie Manén's clear exposition of her solidly grounded theories and well-tried practice will prompt wide, healthy, and positive questioning of established methods, and should serve to bring about a long-overdue revolution in that least-regulated of all professions, the teaching of singing.

BRIAN TROWELL
Heather Professor of Music
Oxford University

CONTENTS

PREAMBLE

by Professor Dr Jobst Fricke
(translated by Brian Trowell)

Mme Manén deserves high praise for her researches into the vocal technique of Bel Canto and its physical functioning, and for the way in which her untiring investigations, firmly grounded in her own personal experience, have enabled her to propose conclusions in this area which are truly pioneering in character. The Bel Canto teaching manuals have hitherto seemed to enshrine a mystery whose essence must have been passed on by word of mouth from one generation of teachers to another: it is solely thanks to her exhaustive and many-sided researches that we are now in a position to understand and reconstruct their methods. Her work illuminates the purpose underlying the Bel Canto exercises, which was designed to teach the student a specialized type of physical adjustment with a use of the larynx quite different from the normal. It is through the Bel Canto method itself that her book communicates its insights into the sounds and sensations that we experience when singing.

Mme Manén's exertions have breathed new life into a tradition which can be traced down to our own times through only a few lines of descent. Her book subjects to analysis the mental images, feelings, and bodily experiences that accompany phonation, partly because they are anatomical facts and partly in order to attain purely pedagogical ends. From this we are forced to conclude that there is a distinction to be made between the physical functions of Bel Canto singing, in which the ventricular mechanism plays the essential part, and those of normal singing, where it is only the vocal-cord mechanism that comes into play. To establish this antithesis between the mere vocal-cord mechanism and

the ventricular mechanism, which permits one to produce
the full variety of colourings characteristic of Bel Canto, is
indeed the principal aim of her work.

The question remains—which each must answer according
to his own preference in the matter of timbre—whether Bel
Canto is a style of singing still worth striving after in our
own day, whether it accords with modern ideals of timbre.
It is a question which must be asked anew in every age and
of every interpreter. The answers lie in that field of
interplaying tensions between the poles of absolute truth to
the work on the one hand, and of contemporary taste on the
other. If however one's aim is simply to revive a fast-
disappearing technique and to place it at the disposition of
our modern vocal culture, then the question is plainly not
a decisive one. The essential point is that the technique of
Bel Canto offers unrivalled opportunities for achieving the
fullest control of the vocal organs and makes possible a
flexible voice-production unusually rich in those varied
colourings which constitute the unique timbres of classical
Italian art-song.

JOBST FRICKE
Head of the Department of Musical Acoustics
Institute of Musicology
University of Cologne

1 · Introduction

Long before I thought of becoming a professional singer, I knew how to sing. I had learned it as a young girl, not through any systematic instruction, but from my grandmother, in much the same way as children learn to speak by listening to what goes on around them.

My grandmother was an excellent pianist. She had been taught singing by an Italian, Signora Buri, and possessed a beautiful soprano voice. One day, when walking and singing by the sea, she had attracted the attention and admiration of Hermann Levi, who had been appointed Director of the Court Orchestra in Munich by King Ludwig II of Bavaria. Later, at the invitation of Richard Wagner, he was to conduct the first performance of *Parsifal* in Bayreuth. He and Count Hülsen, the Intendant of the Prussian Court Theatre, tried to engage my grandmother for the Opera. But this her father's bourgeois prejudices would not permit; and after she was widowed at the age of twenty-eight, with four children to raise, he always dissuaded her from remarriage.

So my grandmother devoted herself enthusiastically to her interests in music and literature. Together with Siegfried Ochs she founded the Berlin Philharmonic Choir, which was later to be conducted by Otto Klemperer. The leading artists of the time used to meet in her music-room. And it was there that, at the age of nine or ten, I made my début. My grandmother had asked the singer Ethelka Gerster, well known in her day, to sing for her guests the *mezza voce* song 'Meinem Kinde' by Richard Strauss—no easy undertaking! Ethelka declared that it was too hard, and declined. Thereupon I called out pertly, 'But I can sing it!'—and did so too, delighting my grandmother, and receiving much applause!

1

Even when I was married and the mother of two children, I kept up my singing practice by taking regular lessons with the tenor Julius Lieban, of Bayreuth fame. Eventually I was persuaded to embark on professional training. This was at the urging of the celebrated violinist Carl Flesch, who used to play chamber music with my father and was later to teach at the Curtis Institute in Philadelphia. Erich Kleiber also encouraged me, and this made it easier for me to leave Julius Lieban.

Carl Flesch, convinced that I had the talent to make a career in singing, secured an introduction for me to Anna Schoen-René. It was only then, when I was already in my late twenties, that I received my real professional training. Anna Schoen-René used to teach for half the year in Berlin and for the remainder in New York, where she also sang at the Metropolitan Opera. Later she became a professor of singing at the famous Juilliard Institute in New York.

Anna Schoen-René had been a pupil of Pauline Viardot, one of the renowned opera singers and teachers of the last century. The daughter of a high-ranking Prussian royal forester, she was originally given a scholarship by Kaiser Wilhelm II. At first she studied in Paris with Mathilde Marchesi. The latter, who was married to the well-known Italian tenor Salvatore Marchesi, was widely regarded as an outstanding teacher of the classical Italian school, though in fact she had been born Mathilde Graumann in Frankfurt-on-Main and had received her early training in Vienna. Disappointed by Madame Marchesi, Anna Schoen-René sought and received permission from the Kaiser to continue her studies in Paris with Pauline Viardot.

Pauline Viardot was a daughter of Manuel Vicente del Popolo Garcia (1775–1832). He was the most famous tenor and teacher of his time; his friend Rossini had composed for him the part of Almaviva in *The Barber of Seville*. Born in Spain, he had studied in Naples and then come with his family to Paris, where he eventually set up the École Garcia. Here singers were trained as they were in Naples, according to the traditions of the classical Italian school.

Pauline appeared in Paris, London, New York, Mexico,
Rome, and in St Petersburg, where she became a friend of
Turgenev, late
'crowned with
Franco-Prussia
Turgenev and I
taught, both p
to the methods

The techniq
Pauline Viardo
developed du
development o
classical Italia
Naples, and lar
end of the last
Canto. The ter
Italian schools,
known who co
never mentione
the course of studying literature on the subject. It has never
been clearly defined; it does not mean simply 'beautiful
singing'. Following current practice, I use it to describe the
particular art of voice-production by which the distinctive
timbres of the classical Italian school of singing can be
achieved.

With the development of Bel Canto, singers acquired a
unique ability to develop as outstanding soloists. The unusual
timbres and limpid production that they acquired, together
with their *messa di voce* and coloratura, made their singing
of operatic arias famous outside Italy.

The tuition of Bel Canto was not based on any explicit
theoretical method. Its teachers, the maestri, were
themselves expert performers. They instructed their pupils
in the same way that they themselves had learned, by trial
and error, until their pupils were able to achieve the right
vocal quality. This entirely empirical method, with its
unremitting process of trial and correction, relied heavily on
the accuracy of the pupil's hearing and the acute ear of the

teacher. Because of this, and because they did not make their art explicit, the maestri were suspected of using their teaching method to protect a professional secret. This secret I have succeeded in unravelling.

My own career as a singer began in Berlin in 1930, when I made my début at the Metropole Theatre in the leading role of the operetta *Victoria und ihr Husar*. After this I was engaged by Max Reinhardt for *The Tales of Hoffmann* and *La Belle Hélène*, under the direction of Leo Blech. On tour with the Musikbühne Erbprinz Reuss, I subsequently sang Cherubino and the Countess in *Figaro* in many towns in Germany, including Leipzig. Here the Generalmusikdirektor Gustav Brecher heard me, and immediately engaged me in April 1932 as Lyric Soprano for the Leipzig Opera.

I appeared in England for the first time at the opening of the Glyndebourne opera house in 1934, when I sang Cherubino under Fritz Busch and Carl Ebert. I was also a soloist in BBC broadcasts and in the Albert Hall with the London Philharmonic Orchestra. Later, touring with the Universal Grand Opera under the pseudonym Elza Russell, I sang Marguerita, Nedda, Micaela, and Gilda, as well as the three female parts in *The Tales of Hoffman* at each performance. I was also much in demand, especially as a *Lieder* singer, for concerts and radio broadcasts in Holland, Switzerland, Vienna, and Prague, until my career was interrupted by the outbreak of the Second World War, when I was in London.

During the war I qualified as physiotherapist; I practised and taught in London at Guy's Hospital and the British School of Osteopathy. Meanwhile I had decided that after the war I would become a singing teacher, and started to prepare myself for that profession. I studied all the books that I could find in the British Museum (now British Library) on singing, voice-production, and breathing. Much to my surprise, I soon realized that almost nothing that I read agreed with what I myself did and sensed when I was singing. Were my reservations about authors and authorities well founded? Gradually I became more and more convinced that they were, especially when I read the words of the noted physiologist

Lord E. D. Adrian: 'Sensations are facts to be reckoned with'. This strengthened my resolve to trust my kinaesthetic sense, which had developed through my knowledge and experience of physiotherapy and enabled me to evaluate my sensations.

Thus equipped, after the war, I began to give singing lessons, both privately and in courses in Tottenham for the Middlesex County Council. None the less I still could not rest content, nor cease my attempts to discover how and why my own voice-production seemed diametrically opposed to that put forward in textbooks which appeared to be scientifically based.

A fortunate chance brought me into contact with the octogenarian Dr George Cathcart, an ear, nose, and throat (ENT) specialist and former consultant to the Royal Academy of Music. He had studied classical Italian singing in Naples with Scafati, whose own teacher had been Crescentini, one of the last of the celebrated castrati. Scafati had given Dr Cathcart a book of exercises by the Bel Canto maestro Alessandro Busti, *Studio di canto: Metodi classici del Conservatorio Reale di Napoli*, first published in 1865. It was one of the first textbooks of its kind, and consisted entirely of vocal exercises. It is today out of print. Dr Cathcart kept his copy under his pillow, like a precious relic!

Dr Cathcart interpreted Busti's exercises for me just as Scafati had taught him. Most significant of all was how Busti had begun with a group of basic exercises, the *vocalizzi*, intended as a preparation for the main Bel Canto exercises. Dr Cathcart emphasized repeatedly the special function of the larynx and the special breath-control required for producing the particular Bel Canto timbres. Finally he made me a present of the book, saying, as if he were giving his most treasured possession, 'Now do something with it! It will make you a millionaire! Here is the authentic teaching of the classical Italian School.'

Dr Cathcart also introduced me to a second Bel Canto manual. Another famous teacher, Gaetano Nava of Milan, had published a series of vocal exercises complete with explanations, *Metodo pratico di vocalizzazione*.[1] As with Busti's work, the title already made clear the importance of the *vocalizzi* as basic preparations for the main Bel Canto exercises, the *messa di voce, vibrazione*, etc.

By learning the 'true' Bel Canto teaching from Dr Cathcart and from the exercises of Busti and Nava, I became aware at last that the method I had originally been taught was, in fact, that of Bel Canto. Further investigations in the British Museum led me to the French anatomist Antoine Ferrein. In 1741, while dissecting corpses, he had discovered in the centre of the larynx two 'shelves', reaching horizontally into it. On the assumption — in itself quite understandable — that, during breathing, air is pressed from the lungs towards these folds as though from bellows, Ferrein concluded that speech and song were produced entirely by the vibration of the vocal cords, induced by air pressure from the lungs. Accordingly he named the bands of muscles that he had discovered *cordes vocales*. He assumed that, unless they were set into vibration in this way, the vocal cords in a living person would remain in the horizontal position in which he had observed them in his dissected larynx. Ferrein's explanation of the production of vocal sound received widespread dissemination and recognition.[2]

His theory I call 'vocal-cord production'. It is still put forward, virtually unaltered, in all teaching manuals on the subject, together with the explanation that range, volume, and tone quality are all decisively affected by the resonances above the larynx.[3] But Ferrein had also observed that 'street-singers in Paris and choral singers in the provinces produce their tone not only by means of the invisible vocal cords,

---

[1] Milan, n.d. [1876?].

[2] Antoine Ferrein, 'De la formation de la voix de l'homme', *Mémoires de l'Académie Royale des Sciences* (Paris, 1741), p. 422.

[3] A. Bouhuys, J. Mead, D. F. Proctor and K. N. Stevens, 'Pressure-flow Events during Singing', *Annals of the New York Academy of Sciences*, 155 (1968), 165–76; Bouhuys, Mead, and Proctor, 'Mechanisms generating Subglottic Pressure', ibid., 177–81. See also Bouhuys, Mead, and Proctor, 'Kinetic Aspects of Singing', *Journal of Applied Physiology*, 21 (1966), 483–96.

but—as can be observed externally by their necks—also by use of other parts of the larynx'.[4]

Some hundred years later, Manuel Garcia jun., son of the above-mentioned Manuel Vicente del Popolo Garcia and brother of Pauline Viardot, amazed singers and doctors everywhere by inventing the laryngoscope, a device which enables one to see down the throat into the larynx.

The inventor of this instrument, which is indispensable today for doctors, was in fact a *chanteur manqué*. He had been trained in Bel Canto by his father, who frequently treated him harshly—and even beat him up—but to no avail. While his sister Pauline, and also his other sister Maria (Malibran), became world famous for their singing (though Maria was to die at the age of twenty-eight as the result of a riding accident), Garcia jun. was a failure. At his first appearance in New York with his father's World Touring Italian Opera he was hissed off the stage because of his vocal tremolo. In consequence of this he fell victim to stage fright and, at the age of twenty-three, gave up singing.

Determined to compensate for his misfortune, Garcia jun. enlisted in the French army and set out for the conquest of Algeria. He returned home victorious, and was again accepted by his family. His father allowed him to be his assistant at the École Garcia. Consumed with jealousy at the fame of his father and sisters, he attempted to discover the cause of his own failure as a singer. He took up the vocal-cord theory of Ferrein, and made some dilettantish experiments on the dissected larynxes of chickens, ducks, geese and other poultry, in which he produced sounds with bellows. These naïve pseudo-scientific tests understandably brought him no further. But when he noticed a dentist using a long-handled mirror, he had the idea of constructing a double-mirror laryngoscope. He now boasted of being the first man to have

[4] Ferrein, op. cit., p. 429; see also p. 430: 'Les gens que nous entendons chanter dans les rues de Paris, et au lutrin dans nos provinces, ne font souvent aucun usage ni de la glotte, ni des cordes vocales que nous avons décrites; ils se servent d'un nouvel organe que j'ai découvert, et dont j'ai eu grand soin de constater l'existence.'

observed his own larynx. What he saw led him to the false
conclusion that he had proved the vocal-cord theory. He must
certainly have seen the vocal cords in a horizontal position,
as described by Ferrein. But lacking our present-day knowledge
of anatomy and physiology, he was unaware that the insertion
of the laryngoscope into the throat had completely upset its
various parts. In their natural state the vocal cords lie turned
upwards against the walls of the larynx, as I discovered
through X-ray investigations at the Nuffield Institute for
Medical Research in Oxford. When the laryngoscope is
inserted, the vocal cords are forced down and lie in a
horizontal position.

Nevertheless, Garcia's world-famous invention of the
laryngoscope (made public in 1855) conferred upon his earlier
writings a 'scientific' authority they did not deserve. After his
father's death in 1832, he had taken over his famous singing
school in Paris, the École Garcia, and assumed, without
justification, his father's great reputation as a teacher. In 1840,
under the already widely known name of Garcia, he published
his first manual of singing, *Traité complet de l'art du chant*. In
this, thinking that he knew better, he deliberately altered the
Bel Canto teaching of his father, 'in order that instruction can
be sustained by physiology and directed [on the basis of the
vocal-cord theory] more clearly and completely'. All this was
received with uncritical acceptance. But by making his
alterations, Garcia jun. had mutilated the traditional Bel Canto
method of teaching singing for which the pupils of the École
Garcia had become famous. He had placed the basic exercises
for the 'start of the sound'—the preparation for the principal
Bel Canto exercises—not at the beginning, as Busti and Nava
did, but only as a later exercise.

Owing no doubt to his total preoccupation with the vocal-
cord theory, the inventor of the laryngoscope made no
mention at all in his singing manuals of the special manner
of using the upper air-passages which was a first principle
of Bel Canto technique and teaching. In order to discover
for myself whether Garcia jun. had, in his teaching of
individuals, given any instruction on the use of these upper

air-spaces, I consulted one of his last pupils, Mr Sterling
Mackinlay (author of *Garcia the Centenarian and his
Times*),[5] who has since died. Already confined to a
wheelchair, he assured me that Garcia had never said
anything as to how the upper air-spaces should be used in
order to achieve Bel Canto voice-production.

In 1856, now becoming increasingly famous as the inventor
of the laryngoscope, Garcia published a new version of his
tutor, *Nouveau traité sommaire de l'art du chant*. With this
he was acknowledged as the foremost maestro di canto in
Europe. But at the same time it aroused fierce opposition from
his French colleagues. This may ultimately have been the
reason for his move to London, where the name Garcia had
long been famous through his father's performances.

On his hundredth birthday Garcia received the highest
accolades for his invention of the laryngoscope—but not for
his teaching of singing. These honours included letters
from King Edward VII, the Kaiser, and King Alfonso of
Spain, as well as addresses from some sixteen professional
laryngological societies. Yet it is not recorded if any of his
pupils at the Royal Academy of Music, where he had taught
from 1848, subsequently became famous. Sir Charles Santley
received his basic training from Gaetano Nava in Milan, and
worked with Garcia only later on.

The results of Garcia's teaching were to cause confusion
among singing teachers everywhere. It went unnoticed that
in his last publication, the *Hints on Singing* of 1894, Garcia
had rejected the basis of his own teaching. He now asserted
that the 'start of the sound', which he called the 'coup de
glotte', was to be made 'without impulse of the air'—that
is, without air pressure from the lungs. The unfortunate fact
remains, however, that the widespread recognition of Garcia
as a singing teacher, which arose from his invention of the
laryngoscope, has caused the decline of the classical Italian
school of singing. Certain well-known singers such as Walter
Widdop and Brian Cochlan, who attempted to produce the

[5] Edinburgh and London, 1908.

particular timbres of Bel Canto with the vocal-cord mechanism advocated by Garcia, collapsed on the platform. If air is forced from the lungs as though from bellows, the blood circulation to the heart is interrupted and, with a poor heart condition, this can cause cardiac failure.

In 1832, living in the shadow of the École Garcia in Paris, the Italian Francesco Bennati published his findings on investigations into the voice, 'Du mécanisme de la voix humaine pendant le chant'.[6] Bennati, unlike Garcia, was neither a *chanteur manqué* nor an amateur in the field of medical research. He had an international reputation as an ENT surgeon, and held honorary doctorates from the universities of Paris, London, Edinburgh, Vienna, and elsewhere. In addition, he was a highly skilled singer of Bel Canto, trained by the famous Gasparo Pacchierotti. As a result of his investigations he concluded that there must be two different mechanisms for voice-production in the larynx: 'voix ordinaire', the normal speaking voice, which can also be employed for singing; and 'voix orotunde', in which the great singers of his time had been trained, and with which the great singers produced 'a better quality of tone'. Bennati continued: 'One must rely not only on external observations and hearing in order to ascertain where the sound is produced, whether by the vocal cords or by organs adjacent to them in the larynx. I have made certain experiments which may stimulate others, more capable than myself, to discover fresh knowledge.' The necessary ability is not inborn in man. Yet by using cineradiology and other modern devices for physiological research, I have succeeded in establishing the working of the larynx for singing, continuing Bennati's work and discovering 'fresh knowledge'.

---

[6] *Mémoire* read to the Académie Royale des Sciences, Paris, on 25 Jan. 1830; revised version printed in *Recherches sur le mécanisme de la voix humaine* (Paris, 1832), reprinted in *Études physiologiques et pathologiques sur les organes de la voix humaine* (Paris, 1833).

2 · Investigation of Bel Canto Voice-production and Breath-control

Two hundred years before Ferrein, Leonardo da Vinci, in his characteristic search for knowledge, had experimented — as Garcia jun. was later to do — on the excised larynxes and windpipes of corpses, in order to discover how the human voice was produced. He came to the conclusion that when 'the lung be filled with air and then closed rapidly one will be able to see immediately in what way the pipe known as the trachea produces this sound'.[1] To this the work of Ferrein added the discovery of vocal cords, and the theory that many singers also use other parts of the larynx. Bennati, who, as both singer and doctor, was the first really qualified investigator, concluded, as we have shown above, that there were two different mechanisms of voice-production.

I have followed up these leads. On the basis of *Gray's Anatomy*[2] and Sir Victor Negus's *The Mechanism of the*

---

[1] See E. MacCurdy, ed., *The Notebooks of Leonardo da Vinci* (London, 1938), i. 104: 'Rule to see how the sound of the voice is produced in the front of the trachea. This will be understood by separating this trachea together with the lung of the man, and if this lung be filled with air and then closed rapidly one will be able immediately to see in what way the pipe called the trachea produces this sound; and this can be perceived and heard well in the neck of a swan or a goose which often continues to sing after it is dead.' (*Dell'Anatomia*, fo. A 3ʳ) See also ibid., p. 186: 'The extension and restriction of the trachea together with its dilation and contraction are the cause of the variation of the voice of the animals from high to deep and from deep to high; and as regards the second of these actions, as the shortening of the trachea is not sufficient when the voice is raised it dilates itself somewhat towards the top part, which does not receive any degree of sound but produces a raising of the voice of this remnant of the shortened pipe.' (*Quaderni*, IV, fo. 10ᵛ).

[2] 28th edn., London, 1942.

Larynx,[3] I carried out numerous experiments on myself and my pupils, using vocal exercises, at the Nuffield Institute for Medical Research in Oxford. I discovered that there are indeed two mechanisms for voice-production in singing, each with quite distinct tonal characteristics, namely (*a*) the vocal-cord mechanism, which I named after Ferrein's theory, and (*b*) the ventricular mechanism, so designated by me because the *ventriculum morgagni* (named after its discoverer) is of special importance for the production and variation of Bel Canto timbres.

In October 1946, at the suggestion of Professor Dennis Fry, head of the Department of Phonetics at University College London, who had studied singing with me, I presented my thesis to a group of experts under the chairmanship of the physicist Sir Richard Paget, who had written the authoritative textbook *Human Speech*.[4] Encouraged by Sir Richard, and with the support of Sir Hugh Cairns, a neurosurgeon at the University of Oxford, I submitted my theory for investigation to the Nuffield Institute for Medical Research in Oxford. The X-ray films made there with myself and my pupils as subjects brought forward new knowledge, and confirmed my theory of the two vocal mechanisms and the specificity of their functioning. My research at the University of London Institute of Laryngology and Otology also produced new findings on respiration for singing.[5]

Since 1946 I have extended and completed this basic research through investigation at the Department of Phonetics, University College, London; the Department of Physics, Chelsea Polytechnic; the institutes of phonetics at the universities of Bonn and Münster; the Siemens laboratories in Berlin and Erlangen; the Technische Hochschule, Aachen; and IRCAM (Centre Pompidou), Paris

---

[3] London, 1929.
[4] London, 1930. The committee consisted of Sir Richard Paget, FSP, D H. Lowery (South West Essex Technical College, Walthamstow), Dr W H. George (Chelsea Polytechnic), and Mr Nightingale (BBC Research Department).
[5] See Appendix.

These investigations with modern scientific equipment were the first of their kind.[6] In the course of them, and owing to too-frequent exposure to radiation, I developed a skin cancer (basilion) on my left upper lip, which required surgical removal. The results of my research, which have been checked and approved by specialists, are incorporated in the following chapters.

In 1947 I consulted Professor A. Gemelli, head of the Laboratory of Experimental Research, Università del Sacro Cuore, Milan, who was the first person of authority with whom I discussed my investigations. Through electro-acoustic and radiological tests, he had established that the timbres of the vowels 'a', 'i', and 'oo', modified by the adjustment of the ventricle of Morgagni (as he had heard them sung in La Scala), 'are produced above the vocal cords without the assistance of the lips' (private communication). He confirmed my theory that the Bel Canto timbres on all vowels are based on spontaneous exclamations, themselves derived from primitive human sound.

My theory that in Bel Canto voice-production the larynx is activated from the trigeminal region of the face, as though from a switchboard, is based on a finding of the late Professor Ulrich Ebbecke, a physiologist at the University of Bonn. By means of experiments on himself and his students he had established that, if the upper part of the face is immersed in a bowl of water at a temperature of approximately 18 °C, a reflex opening and closing of the larynx takes place once every second. I then carried out such experiments on myself and my pupils. These were tested and verified in 1979, at my suggestion and in my presence, by Professor Giovanni Cavagna, a physiologist at the University of Milan.

My findings are based on the fact that every human voice possesses a timbre of its own, and that this can be varied towards a higher, lower, louder, or softer emission. The voice, moreover, is a unique instrument. From earliest times it has

---

[6] B. Raymond Fink, *The Human Larynx: A Functional Study* (New York, 1975), p. 61.

been the vehicle used to express human feelings—joy,
sorrow, love, and fear, as well as reactions to external
stimuli—astonishment, horror, dislike, and hatred. This
capacity of the voice was to serve as the model in designing
the various wind and string instruments that make up the
modern orchestra. But instruments made by hand or in a
factory have never been able to achieve the same flexibility,
and instrumental performers have striven after this in vain.

The significant difference between the vocal-cord
mechanism and the ventricular mechanism has been
demonstrated by me in a sound-proof studio and tested by
the physicist Professor Jobst Fricke, the head of the
Department of Musical Acoustics in the University of
Cologne Institute of Musicology, using a Nicolet 660A digital
analyser. Following these experiments, Professor Fricke stated
(private communication):

These tests offered the valuable advantage of comparing the
acoustical findings on the ventricular mechanism on the one hand
with the vocal-cord mechanism on the other, with both produced
by the same subject. Particularly distinct conditions therefore
resulted, since these findings were not overlaid by features resulting
from different subjects.

Generally speaking it became evident that when notes are sung
with the ventricular mechanism (as compared with notes sung
without it), vowel formants shift to lower frequencies, and the
'singing formant' (so called by F. Winckel and J. Sundberg)
concentrates within the region 2700 to 4300 Hz. For instance, with
the vowel 'i', sung on c♯″ or d″, the second harmonic exceeds the
third in strength, and with the fifth harmonic, which allows one
clearly to recognize the singing formant, the spectrum suddenly
breaks off.

This establishes that [while singing with the ventricular
mechanism] lower harmonics stand out more strongly and the
series of harmonics above the singing formant ends rather suddenly,
whereas otherwise [singing with the vocal-cord mechanism] the
overtones above the higher vowel formants decrease in strength the
higher they lie, without contour and without a sharp cut-off point.

Professor Fricke's tests have established scientific evidence
that the two different mechanisms of voice-production for

singing which I have demonstrated produce two highly different sound analyses, and that the ventricular mechanism produces the fuller timbres of Bel Canto singing.

The ventricular mechanism is the particular instrument for which classical Italian music was composed and with which alone classical Italian music should be sung, just as a violin sonata must be played, and can be played adequately, only with a violin.

During the summer of 1976 I had the opportunity to discuss my work in Paris with Professor Jacques de Lattre, the head of the Department of Human Physiology at the Sorbonne, and subsequently with him and Professor Arend Bouhuys, Yale University, who was in Paris at that time. In our joint session I demonstrated to them the specific form of breath-control necessary for Bel Canto, as studied with Mr Nigel Edwards (see p. 44). After extended discussion, Professor Bouhuys acknowledged that he was convinced by my theory, and declared that the experiments into respiration for singing that he had conducted some years before in the USA must now be carried out again 'from scratch', but this time with singers trained in Bel Canto, who had not been available to him then. As editor of one of the most important works on respiration, *Breathing: Physiology, Environment and Lung Disease*,[7] he then proposed that, jointly with himself, I should present the results of my work at the next International Congress of Physiologists. Only in February 1980, when I sent him a preliminary draft of this work, did I learn from his assistant that he had died suddenly in June 1979.

---

[7] New York, 1971, revised and enlarged, 1974.

3 · Characteristics of Bel Canto

Singing is an expression of human emotion—of joy or sorrow—which arises from inner feeling or external stimulus. People from all nations have their own ways of expressing their emotions in song, but this ability has been particularly given to Italians, many of whom have beautiful natural voices. Through this gift, and through the artistic and social traditions that arose to allow its expression, they have been able to produce the famous Bel Canto composers and solo singers. In the streets of Naples, a city which during the Baroque period was famous for its classical singing schools, one can still hear mendicant street-singers singing popular operatic arias, attentively listened to from windows and alleyways by a song-loving public. This public has always been aware of the superlative art that enabled the virtuosi and prima donnas of the San Carlo Opera to sing popular operatic arias with the affecting timbres characteristic of Bel Canto. Despite what has often been said, it was not, and is not, the perennial blue skies that make the Italians lovers of singing: it is rather the extrovert urge they have to express all the shades of their feelings and emotions in song. The mastery of Bel Canto shown by virtuosi and prima donnas seemed supernatural, and was therefore regarded as a magic art. In order to hear it, impoverished Neapolitans would forgo their meals to secure standing-room in 'their' San Carlo Opera.

Giulio Caccini (c.1545–1618) played a special part in the development of the solo voice in Bel Canto composition. Before his voice broke he was a treble singer in the choir of the Julian Chapel in Rome. Here he attracted the attention of Cardinal Fernando de' Medici, who took him to Florence, where he received further tuition in composition and singing

17

from Scipione della Palla. He became one of the most accomplished tenors of his time. In 1579 he had a spectacular success when he sang at the wedding of the Archduke Francisco de' Medici and Bianca Cappello. Subsequently he became the most sought-after singing teacher in Florence.

As a virtuoso soloist in the Camerata of Count Giovanni de' Bardi, Caccini became that academy's authority on singing technique for the solo voice. The members of this group sought to develop new methods of composing for the solo voice, based on their investigations into the music of the ancient Greeks, in which solo voices were already pre-eminent for their natural ability to express human emotions. This ability Caccini assimilated with enthusiasm in his compositions, and in February 1602 (new style) he published a book of songs, *Le nuove musiche*.[1] In his foreword he was the first to describe the principles used in his vocal compositions and the technique needed to sing them. Until that time, singers sang (mainly) in consort, thereby 'subduing human passions through the refinement of their art'. In contrast to this, the new compositions of Caccini were intended to arouse all kinds of emotion in the listeners. Soloists now had to stand out from the accompanying instruments so that, by imitating the powers of expression shown in rhetoric and the declamation of actors — and in the music of the Greeks — they could bring to full expression the special property of the human voice: to portray a variety of emotions in correspondingly varied vocal timbres.

Like all singing teachers of his time, Caccini seems to have taught in the manner also adopted by the later masters of the classical Italian schools of the eighteenth and nineteenth centuries. They first of all gave a demonstration, then listened with a finely tuned ear while the pupil imitated it, making continual corrections until the pupil was able to achieve the correct production and quality of timbre. From the beginning, they knew that the singing voice functioned from the larynx:

[1] Florence, 1601 (old style).

'cantare con la gorga'. Caccini, however, brought forward fresh knowledge for solo voice-production by stressing the importance of the 'start' of the sound, to which 'a crescendo is to be joined'. Thereby, the voice became 'delightful' in every register and timbre.

Caccini had no knowledge of the anatomical configuration of the larynx, nor of the physiology of voice-production. It is only in recent times that we have been able to acquire such knowledge, through investigations using modern scientific equipment and instruments such as X-ray cine-film machines. The knowledge thus revealed has established that Caccini, with his description of the importance of the 'start' of the sound and the variety of timbres necessary for accomplished Bel Canto singing (using the ventricular mechanism), was an important precursor in the development of Bel Canto technique.[2]

The extraordinary power and effectiveness of this manner of singing is shown by the reaction of the audience, who now shared the emotions that the singer was expressing in accordance with the composer's intentions. Many composers of classical Italian music were themselves trained singers, and were therefore intimately aware of the capacities and limitations of the voice in giving expression to human moods. With their southern sensitivity they could easily assimilate the emotions of both simple and complex characters, and represent these in colourful sounds, just as painters mix every shade of colour on their palettes. They sought the timbres for their arias from the spectrum of primeval sounds with which peoples of the Western world have always expressed their feelings and moods. When describing an event with little emotional content, the low middle register of the voice is employed. But if the emotion to be expressed is to be intensified, the vocal register changes significantly. When expressing pleasure, for example, the natural timbre manifests

[2] David Galliver, 'Cantare con la gorga', *Studies in Music*, 7 (1973), 10–18; 'Cantare con affetto', *Studies in Music*, 8 (1974), 1–7; 'The Vocal Technique of Caccini', *Poesia e musica nell'estetica del XVI e XVII secolo* (Florence, 1976), 7–11.

itself in a sound evolved from the corresponding primeval exclamation: 'ah!' ('how lovely!'). The expression of dislike or hatred is denoted in the vowel 'i' (as 'ie' in 'fierce'), the expression of fear and horror in the vowel 'u' (as 'oo' in 'doom'). These symbolic examples can be combined in various ways, according to the inner mood represented by the notes written by the composer.

The more accomplished an artistic performance is on the stage, the simpler its achievement appears to be to the public. Voice-production for classical singing, as it was taught in the schools of Italy, requires a special technique of sound-production and respiration, in addition to the entire physical and psychic participation of the artist. The inner disposition of the Bel Canto singer is reflected in posture, gestures, breathing, and heartbeat. When reacting to a composition, as for instance by singing a phrase, nervous impulses, actuated from the eyes and ears, are carried by the nerves to the elements that control voice-production, i.e. breathing and heartbeat. These impulses stimulate and direct the larynx and the air-passages actually to produce the voice and its timbres. Chemical substances are poured into the bloodstream, thus strengthening the resources in the singer's system, when the increased demands of singing require a heightened awareness.

The special art of Bel Canto singers consisted in their ability to sing musical phrases in every timbre, and to show their mastery of florid singing, not only in the *passaggi* and scales (*scale volate*) which composers demanded in their arias, but also in the expressive ornamentation that singers were expected to add *ex tempore* in the reprise or *da capo* section. This highly accomplished art became possible during the seventeenth century with the development of monody and opera. With this change, solo singers, accompanied by a single instrument or an orchestra, now achieved supremacy over instrumentalists. But they in turn were then impelled to rival the greater compass and dexterity of instrumentalists. In consequence they eventually succeeded in increasing their range, both upwards and downwards, to a span of three octaves; and, above all, they achieved a mastery of coloratura which made classical Italian singing famous everywhere as an insurpassable accomplishment.

Wherein does this extraordinary power and effectiveness of classical Italian singing consist? This question has scarcely ever been examined. No profound psychological analysis, however, is required to find the answer. It consists simply in the aura of psychic energy released through the brilliance of Bel Canto singing, within which public and artists alike feel themselves drawn together as one by the events taking place on the stage.

This musical experience, a unique and total communication between artist and public, cannot be conveyed satisfactorily by radio and television broadcasts, or through the medium of electronic recording. With its multifarious and multicoloured potential for expression, the human voice stands high above all instruments. Nor will it be surpassed by any electronic apparatus that technicians may be able to devise in the name of progress.

Just as our natural environment is being destroyed by much-lauded technical advances, so the advent of the technician has had a negative effect on the world of music. Compositions are no longer basic human reactions, responses to the environment, and the feelings which arise from these. Sounds, note-rows, timbres, noises, and resonances are invented which are all orientated towards rationally devised conceptions. These are fundamentally a travesty of genuine human expression in music and song. The sound-production of electronic instruments has absolutely nothing in common with man's own native endowment, the ability to express feelings and moods, and reactions to these, and to communicate with his fellow men by using the natural timbres of the voice.

At the outset of my research, I had to come to terms with these facts. In 1950, in order to further interdisciplinary aspects of my work, I joined with experts from the universities of Cologne, Bonn, Aachen, and Münster, and founded in Cologne a Society for Sound Research (Gesellschaft für Klangforschung).[3] The physicist Professor Werner Meyer-Eppler, Director of the Institute of Phonetics at the University of Bonn (less well known as the teacher of Stockhausen), readily agreed to my suggestion that we should analyse the acoustic properties of the singing voice. In the process he made me aware of his own ideas on electronic composition. At first I was fascinated by this new technical 'art' of composing with electronic equipment, achieved, as he said, 'through collaboration between a technician and a musician, with the latter having the upper hand'. I became so involved in this musical activity, which was completely new to me, that I persuaded the Director-General of West German Radio, Hans Hartmann (who was married to a friend of mine, the singer Ottilie Schott), to set up an electronic studio. But in the mean time it had dawned upon me that no electronic instrument devised by a technician could ever approach the expressive power of the human voice. I resolved thereupon to devote myself entirely to research into the voice-production of Bel Canto and its principles.

Today the technique of Bel Canto is possessed by only a few. Some are born with it, the 'natural' talents who use the ventricular mechanism quite unconsciously—as, for example, does Placido Domingo, who claims that he learnt to sing on his own without formal tuition. Others have had to acquire their mastery of the classical art of singing through a rigorous course of study, as, for example, Maria Callas had to do. She was a student of singing in Athens with a pupil of mine, Arda Mandikian. Through a fortunate chance she secured the opportunity to sing to Toscanini. She had a good voice and was talented, the maestro told her. But now she must really learn to sing properly. He sent her to Tullio Serafin, conductor of La Scala, who made of her voice what is possible only with the technique and style of Italian artistic singing. Kiri te Kanawa was taught the Italian art of singing by a nun in a convent in New Zealand before she came to Europe. In London she needed to add to her accomplished

---

[3] See Appendix.

Bel Canto technique only the style and interpretation that classical compositions require.

In the course of time, much has changed in the basic structures upon which the principles of Bel Canto were built. Composers and singers of modern times differ in build and motivation from those of the Baroque, whose art has never been surpassed. What composer today can sing a Bel Canto aria? What composer today makes use of the vast palette of timbres which the voice can display using Bel Canto technique—and with that technique alone? For it is only from the primeval sounds and exclamations, with which men express their inner feelings and reactions to impressions from the world around them—joy, surprise, grief, passion, annoyance, anger, hatred, etc.—that the colourful timbres of Bel Canto can emanate. After the flowering of the classical Italian art of singing, the last century saw it decline as a result of the erroneous teaching of Manuel Garcia jun. By using the vocal-cord mechanism, a singer could vary the music composed for him in respect of range and volume; but he was no longer taught to employ any of the timbres of Bel Canto.

Since the introduction of radio, record, and cassette recordings made by singing through a microphone, singers have been subjected to many constraints on their voice-production, which need not be discussed here. A succession of loud and soft sounds replaces the variety of tonal colour offered by the Bel Canto technique. The majority of singers, unaware of the range of different timbres which it is in their power to develop, are content to use only the inborn, apparently 'natural' timbres which depend on their individual physical and psychic make-up: such a singer believes that this is the feature which identifies his or her unique value as an artist ('my' voice). Thus the multiplicity of colour of the Bel Canto technique is quite ignored. The expressive ability of singers is further affected when, instead of standing before an audience, they have to face the blank walls of a studio. Posture, gesture, and movement are forgotten, although these should contribute to the tone-production, and can help evoke in the singer's mind the appropriate timbres of Bel Canto, as well as provide a suitable visual explanation for the audience. But whatever may be asked of singers performing music in the classical style, whatever may be required of them in the future in the way of sophisticated production or microphone techniques: when the need arises to present an authentic interpretation of the whole range of classical compositions, only the master of Bel Canto technique will be able to meet every demand.

4 · Building the Bel Canto Instrument

The singer's instrument consists not only of the larynx, which is usually regarded as the organ of the voice, but of his whole body. In fact, the larnyx is not self-activating, as are, for example, the eyes, which carry out their function of seeing without the help of any other organ. Voice-production for speaking and singing requires a complex co-operation of basic parts of the body, including, in addition to the larynx itself, the resonances in the air-passages. Below the larynx there are the lungs, with their pleurae and bronchi, and the windpipe; and above the larynx, the jaws, mouth cavity, tongue, and nose, as well as the nasal passages with their complex adjacent areas of cartilages and muscles, only some of which are movable.

Students of singing, even when their physical and intellectual development is complete, are not yet qualified to control the instrument for performing Bel Canto. Those who have no defects in their vocal organs can sing in whatever way they please. Such unschooled singers normally use the larynx quite involuntarily, in the manner described by the vocal-cord theory. Anyone can employ this form of production, using his inborn natural voice with its own range and quality, but he will produce a single vocal colour, and not the variety of Bel Canto timbres. Correct voice-production in the classical Italian style can be achieved only when the whole body is used as a resonator, and when the singer possesses the art of bringing together the various elements of his vocal equipment into one harmonious combination.

From the outset, the singer's training must be directed towards this goal. First he must learn to direct and discipline his body. Posture, movement, and gesture will harmonize as the visible expression of the Bel Canto timbres. The whole body needs to be trained, so that it remains fully controlled in every position during singing. This basic training demands a regular physical education of the body, for only in this way can it be prepared as the instrument of Bel Canto. A student of singing does not need detailed anatomical and physiological knowledge such as a medical student must acquire, but he must make himself familiar with the basic parts of his instrument and know their functions. He must learn to recognize these, while at the same time, through his singing, becoming aware of his sensations. These factors are seldom considered or taught by teachers of singing, and thus gifted pupils can have their voices ruined. More than a century ago this was bitterly criticized by Professor Karl Ludwig Merkel, a lecturer in anthropology at Leipzig University.[1]

However successful a singer's career has been, it does not in itself qualify him to teach singing. To teach Bel Canto properly requires interdisciplinary knowledge of anatomy, physiology, and psychology. Manual dexterity is not of the same importance for singers as it is for instrumentalists or sculptors; nor does the singer need, as artists and painters do, impeccable power of vision and sense of visual colour. Under the guidance of his teacher, however, he must build his entire physical, spiritual, and psychological make-up into an instrument. In effecting this, the development of a finely discriminating ear is of special importance. Just as the faculty of hearing, even when it is initially in a normal and healthy condition, can be adversely affected by excessive external noise, so it can also be refined, though the level of possible improvement will vary from one individual to another. What is essential is that acuteness of hearing with which the maestri of the classical Italian school corrected their pupils. This sensitivity is, in varying degrees, an endowment of nature; but, like practically all organic functions, it can be developed and sharpened.

[1] *Der Kehlkopf* (Leipzig, 1873).

(a) Posture

Professional singers, like instrumentalists — even those who play seated — need to acquire good posture. Whereas most instrumentalists can continue to practise their profession until they reach the normal age of retirement, singers, like dancers, find their capacities affected by increasing age. All the same, they too can extend the length of their professional activity if, from the outset, they can keep their physique in the best possible condition. With the help of modern science, this has become possible today for all singers, thanks to Sir Charles Sherrington's discovery of the inborn kinetic reflexes, for which he was awarded the Nobel Prize in 1932. Today, the singer can learn and teach, as I did in my training as a physiotherapist, how to use the muscles so as to gain the greatest possible benefit for the arduous standing and moving before the public that his professional work entails.

Standing, particularly in the military stance, is physically straining, and a correct, and therefore properly relaxed, posture can be adversely affected by modes of fashion — high heels, corsets, etc. — and by repetitious work like sitting at a desk or a conveyor belt. The natural coming and going of everyday life in no way guarantees good posture. In order that the body may be supported easily, the relaxation of countless muscles is necessary. A singer must first be able to achieve complete relaxation in order to bring legs, spine, shoulder-girdle, neck, and head into the correct relationship.

The spine consists of two relatively firm sections and two which are more flexible (see Fig. 1). The firmer sections are:

(1) the chest;
(2) the sacrum, which is embedded in the hip-bone.

The more flexible sections are:

(1) the neck, or cervical spine;
(2) the lower back, or lumbar spine.

In order to bring the body into a state of equilibrium and to retain it, the moving parts must be stretched. The legs, which bear the body's weight, are joined to the pelvis and

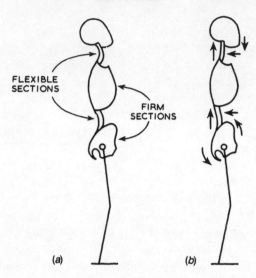

FIG. 1. Posture: (a) before adjustments to the flexible parts of the spine, (b) after correct adjustments

through it connect them to the backbone. Their alignment is effected through the correct disposition of the spine. This is done by placing both forefingers on the upper frontal border of the hip-bones, then, with the thumbs, moving the hip back and forth with rocking movements from the rear, until the frontal part is moved inwards and upwards and the rear part moves easily downwards. This disposition gives the pelvis the correct position of relaxation, with the lower back stretched downwards; the whole body is then extended. The intestines lie completely relaxed, as if in a basket. The stomach becomes flatter, and the entire posture is improved.

The legs, which carry the weight of the body, have three joints: the hip-joint, the knee, and the ankle (see Fig. 2). When the body is lying down, with the legs carrying no weight, every movement of the hip-joint will cause a corresponding movement of the knee, as well as of the upper and lower thigh and feet. These movements are a single functional unity. When standing, with the legs carrying the weight of the body, the optimum position is reached when hip-joint and knee

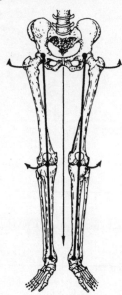

FIG. 2. The hip-bone and leg as weight-bearing column

are turned slightly outwards, with the feet forming an angle of some thirty degrees with the mid-line. Then one observes that the muscles at the back of the thigh are tautened, retaining the hip-bone in correct position. The instep is raised, and the toes and heels grip the ground. The balance of the body will be felt to shift backwards.

Especially flexible and sensitive are the cervical vertebrae of the neck. They can make two quite distinct movements — forwards and backwards, and circular. They can also move the head forwards and backwards in a nodding movement, by means of a small bone, known as the atlas, between the upper neck vertebrae and the skull. The singer obtains the correct position of the neck by stretching it as far as possible backwards and upwards, moving the cervical vertebrae backwards. In doing this the rib-cage is raised. This is of special importance, because it is only in this way that the muscles can hold the larynx and move more freely and in balance in the throat.

The head is supported and moved by the muscles of the neck and chest. The best position is attained when an

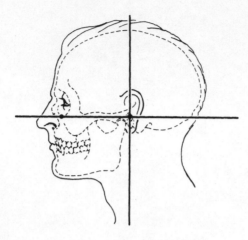

Fig. 3. Balanced position of the head

imaginary line can be drawn, horizontally and parallel to the ground, from the middle of the ear to the lower bones of the eye sockets (see Fig. 3).

The chest, which consists of the ribs and the sternum, attains its correct position through the correct adjustment of the shoulder-girdle. This too is of special importance for the singer, since it is here that the breath required for singing is stored. The shoulder-girdle consists of a pair of bones, right and left, each made up of a shoulder-blade and a collar-bone. The angle on each side between these bones determines the dimensions of the rib-cage from front to back. The maximum space within the rib-cage is obtained by rotating the small joint between the shoulder-blades and the collar-bone. This causes a widening of the rib-cage, and the arms are turned in the shoulder-joints sideways and outwards. In this position one has the feeling of carrying a yoke from which buckets are hanging. The shoulder can be shrugged without interfering with the rib-cage. Thus the greatest elasticity of the body is obtained, alerted and prepared for singing (see Fig. 4).

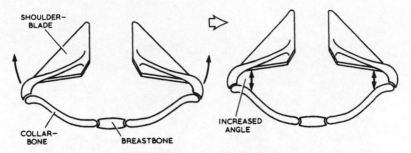

FIG. 4. Adjustments to the shoulder-girdle (seen from above)

(b) The mechanism of the larynx

As stated above, the larynx is not a self-activating organ; yet in voice-production it has a more important function than all other participating parts. Students of singing can refer to textbooks of anatomy for the most comprehensive information about the various components of the larynx. The diagram shown here (Fig. 5) aims only at clarifying those basic elements of the larynx which perform special and individual functions in Bel Canto.

The larynx forms a tubular link between the air-passages above and below it, i.e. between the jaws, nasal spaces, and oral spaces above, and the windpipe, bronchi, and lungs below. It is approximately one and a half to two inches long and two to three inches wide, depending on the build of the individual. Its interior is lined with moist, sticky membrane, and its various cartilages are connected with each other by elastic membranes and ligaments. These can be moved by different muscles, thereby changing their positions and relationships to each other. It is most important for the singer to realize that the disposition of the larynx can change in this way. For the singer the most important parts of the larynx are:

(1) the vocal cords;
(2) the false vocal cords;
(3) the ary-epiglottic folds, between the epiglottis and the cervical vertebrae;
(4) the epiglottis;
(5) the arytenoid cartilages.

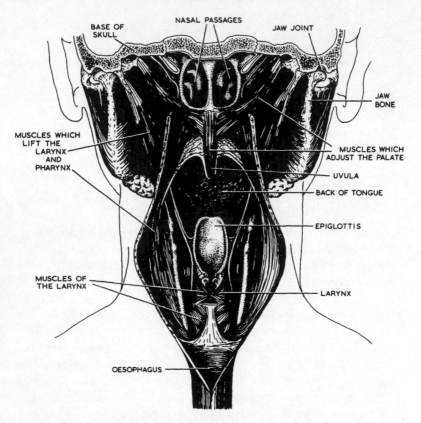

FIG. 5. The vocal instrument viewed from behind (the pharynx is opened to show the larynx and muscles)

In normal breathing, the larynx is open, and air can pass freely in and out. The vocal cords lie upright along the inner side of the larynx. They do not reach horizontally into the larynx, as was thought in the past. This view has now been refuted by X-ray tomograms which I have made (see Fig. 6).[2]

---

[2] These X-ray tomograms were prepared by Dr G. M. Ardran, Dr F. H. Kemp, and the author at the Nuffield Institute for Medical Research, Oxford. See their article 'Closure of the Larynx', *British Journal of Radiology*, 26 (1953), 497–509.

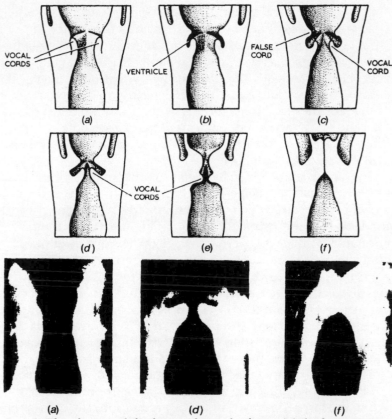

FIG. 6. The closing of the larynx from the front: (*a*) the larynx open during quiet breathing, (*b*) beginning to close, (*c*) and (*d*) the vocal cords and false cords converging towards the centre, (*e*) the larynx narrowed as the vocal cords and false cords nearly meet, (*f*) the larynx closed before the start of the note.

The three tomograms reproduced here show positions (*a*), (*d*), and (*f*).

The ary-epiglottic folds are attached to the arytenoid cartilages and lie obliquely at the sides of the epiglottis. During singing, the vocal cords and the arytenoid cartilages converge towards the centre, closing the entrance and exit to the larynx.

Between the vocal cords and the ary-epiglottic folds lie the false vocal cords. They bulge out towards the centre of the larynx, forming a small sac, the ventricle of Morgagni, between themselves and the vocal cords. During singing, this ventricle is filled with air, allowing free vibration of the vocal cords. The ventricle can alter its length and diameter. On both sides there are folds which, when filled with air, form a small sac, the so-called sacculus. This is a sac with no exit, like the appendix, and fills with air when the specific timbres of Bel Canto are produced.

The larynx is not joined by bones to other parts. Its position in the neck can be changed only by movements of the tongue and of the muscles which connect the larynx to other parts of the body, i.e. the hyoid bone, the skull, and the sternum. In normal breathing, the larynx is open. When one swallows, it closes by reflex, in order to prevent liquid or solid food from passing down into the lower air-passages. This automatic closure of the upper entrance to the larynx is made by the epiglottis. The epiglottis resembles a spoon, its handle extending down along the inner wall of the larynx as far as the vocal cords. When food is ingested, the epiglottis covers the larynx by reflex, preventing food from entering it.

The ary-epiglottic folds, the false vocal cords, and the vocal cords are attached to the arytenoid cartilages in the larynx. When the larynx is closed in voice-production, the cartilages point downwards and inwards to the front.

(c) The resonators

The mechanism of Bel Canto, like that of all musical instruments, has a sound producer as well as resonators. Resonators strengthen certain harmonics of the sound producer and filter out others.

(i) The main resonator of the larynx is the pharyngeal space above the entrance to the larynx and the oesophagus. It consists of the upper naso-pharynx and the middle and lower pharynx behind the tongue. These form the main resonators for laryngeal sounds. Their shape can be altered, in length and width, by the action of straight and round muscles. But these changes cannot easily be controlled by the will: they occur as reflex actions when swallowing. In singing, every shade of dynamics and timbre requires a corresponding shaping of the middle and lower pharynx. This requires patience and practice.

Eminent singers of the past have always stressed the importance of opening up the pharynx, knowing that fine vocal quality depends on it. Tito Schipa, for example, said that while he was singing, an egg might be introduced, without breaking it, over his tongue and into his gullet. Lilli Lehmann had the sensation that her voice stood on a column of air or a fountain.[3] I myself feel as if there is a soap-bubble in my gullet behind my tongue, which alters its shape during singing in relation to the changes in the pharynx.

(ii) The mouth cavity, which is enclosed by the jaws, also acts as a resonator. By nature, the jaws in carnivores are intended for biting vertically, and in herbivorous animals for chewing or grinding horizontally; in humans both functions obtain. The upper jaw is a fixed component of the lower part of the skull, and can be moved only together with the skull. The lower jaw is an oval-shaped bone, open at the rear, known as the mandible. It hangs with the rear hinged to a muscle, known as the pterygoid, at the back of the upper jaw (see Fig. 7). The lower jaw does not move in the same way as other bones, such as the knee or the elbow. In order for the jaw to open, the mandible is released forwards and downwards by the pterygoid muscle. The pterygoid is thereby stretched, and supports the lower jaw, which now hangs weightlessly parallel to the upper jaw. In this position the lower jaw can be moved at will in all directions by the muscles that attach it to the skull. For the singer this horizontal position of the jaw is correct. By opening the jaw in the manner described, the resonating mouth cavities can be altered. If the singer opens his mouth by separating his lips suddenly without first unhinging the mandible, grimaces will be the only result.

---

[3] See Lilli Lehmann, *How to Sing* (New York, 1914), p. 34.

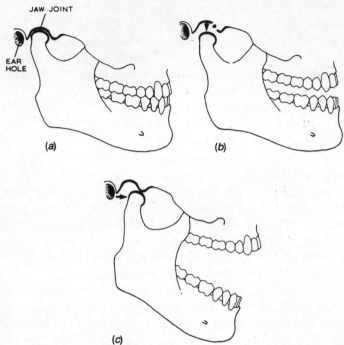

FIG. 7. Movements of the jaw joint: (a) jaw closed, (b) weightless hanging of the lower jaw, (c) jaw fully open

(iii) The inner volume of the nose is greater than it appears externally. The interior of the nose is divided by a vertical septum. Both nostrils open up into a small vestibule, from which two horizontal canals lead into the nose. When one inspires (breathes in), the air passes inwards through the passage formed by the three small bones, the conchae, into the naso-pharynx, and it passes outwards when one expires (breathes out). The entrances to the sinuses are situated in these respiratory canals (see Fig. 8).

The roof of the naso-pharynx consists of the lower cranial bone and its back wall of round muscles, which can extend backwards to enlarge or reduce the volume of the naso-pharynx. The floor of the naso-pharynx consists of the hard palate and its continuation, the soft palate. The latter

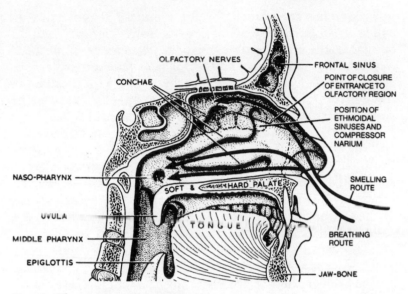

FIG. 8. The upper respiratory tracts

stretches backwards and downwards at an angle of some ninety degrees into the middle pharynx, where the muscles on each side combine to form the uvula.

The entrance to the organ of smell, the ethmoid bone, situated in the upper part of the nose, has a special importance for tone quality. It is connected to the nostrils below by a very narrow passage. In order to prevent the entry of bad or harmful odours or gases during inspiration, a set of small muscles (the compressor narium), acting as a reflex safety-valve, closes off the entrance to the olfactory bulb, the organ of smell. At the same time the larynx is closed reflexly to protect the lungs. This closing mechanism of the compressor narium I call the *imposto*.

Only with the *imposto* mechanism can the vocal timbres of Bel Canto be produced and varied. The closure of the larnyx for starting a sound does not automatically cause a closure of the organ of smell by the compressor narium. However, by using the *imposto* mechanism for the start of the sound, the vocal timbres of Bel Canto can be varied at will. This technique has been taught by the Viennese School and was called *Hochgriff* to distinguish it from *Tiefgriff*, which designates the vocal-cord mechanism. The *Hochgriff* method, in contrast to that of the *Tiefgriff*, has never been explained, although voice-production using the *imposto* mechanism is frequently used—quite unconsciously—by successful singers, particularly the so-called *Naturtalente*.

The start of the sound from the *imposto* should be practised on 'ah' and the brighter 'ee', by means of a scale rising to the fifth and eventually to the octave. The singer should consciously 'switch on' the start of the sound from the *imposto*. This requires a closure by the compressor narium of the entrance to the ethmoid bone before the start of the sound. Lilli Lehmann likened this sensation to having a saddle over the bridge of the nose. Other singers have described it as a feeling of tension, as if a drumhead were being tautened over the bridge of the nose.

5 · Bel Canto Breath-control and Voice-production

In the teaching of singing, respiration has always been considered the most important component in voice-production. A whole series of extremely varied and contradictory theories exists on this subject. In the Italian classical singing schools, the teaching and acquisition of correct breathing for singing was given special importance: 'chi sa respirare sa cantare'. The maestri of Bel Canto left behind no written instructions to clarify this important teaching. From the detailed descriptions that Dr Cathcart gave me of his tuition from Scafati in Naples, however, I was able to deduce that the technique of Bel Canto requires a special form of breath-control. The first criticism made by Scafati of Dr Cathcart's manner of breathing for singing was 'respirate troppo basso' (you are breathing too deeply). From this 'magic formula' which Dr Cathcart passed on to me, it is clear that what Scafati meant by 'respirare' was not the natural breathing innate in all men, but a special method of emitting the breath. This is evident also from the exercises (see p. 5f.) prescribed by Busti and Nava as preparatory to the main Bel Canto exercises. The preceding 'rest' in all these exercises signifies that, to prepare for the 'ah', the breath must first be held, and only then allowed to be emitted. Lilli Lehmann also recommended that the breath be held before beginning to sing.[1] In the classical Bel Canto schools, the various much-vaunted 'exercises for breath-control' that are used today simply did not exist. My own teacher, Anna Schoen-René, who was trained in the tradition of Bel Canto, never drilled me with breathing exercises.

---

[1] *How to Sing*, pp. 26–7.

Natural breathing consists of two phases of approximately the same duration: inspiration and expiration. Both take place through the nose, and in the process the nasal passages and air-spaces are enlarged. During inspiration the rib-cage rises and expands in all directions. The diaphragm descends, the internal organs of the abdomen are pushed downwards, and the stomach flattens. The lungs remain passive, but air is drawn into them through the expansion of the rib-cage (see Figs. 9a and 10a). During expiration the diaphragm rises, and the breathing passages are narrowed (see Figs. 9b and 10b).

The lungs consist of an elastic, spongy tissue; this is enveloped by the pleurae, which comprise the outer and inner pleurae covering the diaphragm. The air in the lungs has a lower pressure than that in the outside atmosphere. The more the rib-cage is enlarged, the more the pressure in the lungs decreases; at the same time the elastic tissue of the lung expands. The air-passages to the lung—the trachea, the bronchi, and their smaller branches—lengthen and widen. Owing to the decrease of pressure in the air-spaces, air is drawn in from outside.

Before the singer can practise correct respiration for Bel Canto, he must learn to observe his own natural breathing. If he finds that his abdomen bulges out during inspiration, his stomach muscles are too flabby. He must then practise to acquire the tautness of the abdominal muscles necessary

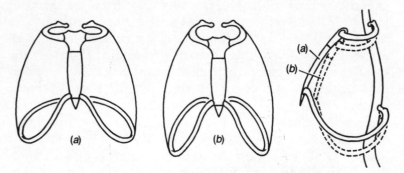

Fig. 9. The rib-cage, seen from behind: (a) after breathing in, (b) before breathing in

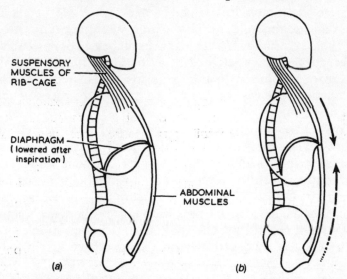

SUSPENSORY
MUSCLES OF
RIB-CAGE

DIAPHRAGM
(lowered after
inspiration)

ABDOMINAL
MUSCLES

(a)   (b)

FIG. 10. Position of the chest, diaphragm, and abdominal wall: (a) after breathing in, (b) during breathing out

for Bel Canto. Two exercises are especially suitable for this purpose:

(1) the singer lies down on a straight surface, lifts his head slowly, and puts it down again slowly;
(2) he lifts his legs slowly from the supporting surface, and puts them down again as slowly as he can, without bending them.

These exercises should be repeated as desired, but without over-exertion.

During these exercises, the singer must observe his internal sensations when he breathes in and out quietly. First of all he should take in as much air as he can — a deep breath. This produces a sensation of fullness and stiffness. Such a full, deep breath is not at all suitable for singing.

In order to understand the correct respiration for singing, the singer should now imagine a short 'scene', and analyse it in slow motion. He enters a room and sees a letter on the table. He picks it up, and looks at the handwriting with surprise: he is nonplussed, he 'stops short'. He opens the letter and begins to read. His expression changes to one of agreeable surprise over a startlingly good piece of news in the letter. He draws a quick breath, as if gasping for air. He holds his breath involuntarily and exclaims, 'ah!' Such a reaction can occur in the case of anyone surprised by a piece of good news.

This exclamatory 'ah!', as opposed to a spoken 'a', embodies the particular vocal timbre expressing the mood aroused in the reader of the letter by his good news. The timbre of this 'ah!' is produced by a reflex, controlled by a primitive respiratory centre of the brain, the bulba, and resembles the first cry of a new-born child. The speech-centre of the brain controlling the spoken 'a' develops much later, in the respiratory centre within the fourth ventricle of the brain.

The pitch of the 'ah!' will vary—as will the pitches of the other variable timbres—according to the intensity of the inner mood that the surprise evokes. If one is not much affected, the 'ah!' will be light and soft, in the lower middle range of the natural voice. But if the feeling of joyful surprise is more intense, the pitch of the 'ah!' will be significantly louder, and may be a third, a fourth, a fifth, or even an octave higher in pitch.

This state of being aroused or startled is produced by a reflex action which affects the whole system. It was investigated experimentally by the English physiologist Robert McNairn Wilson. His conclusions, published in *The Hearts of Man*,[2] are given below in abbreviated form.

The subject's facial expression changes from one of indifference to one of agreeable surprise, in which the whole system participates. In physical terms:

(1) he draws a quick breath; his larynx closes, he holds his breath;

(2) his jaws separate and are kept horizontal;

(3) his chest is lifted, the abdomen is flattened;

---

[2] London, 1918.

(4) his cheeks are lifted, the nasal space is widened;
(5) his eyebrows are raised, his eyes open.

Now the singer gives expression to his joyful reaction to this agreeable surprise:

(6) his larynx opens, he exclaims, 'ah!'; the larynx closes. The jaws remain separated, the chest remains lifted.

These reactions cause a condition of intense, alert concentration. In normal daily life, the snatched breath occurs as a result of a variety of stimuli: through fear, for example, and especially when attempting to master difficult movements of the body or when struggling with a demanding manual task—e.g. threading a needle—or when working carefully with delicate instruments. This is also what happens with the singer: whenever he is confronted with a vocal entry, he must take a snatched breath and rouse himself into a state of alert, concentrated preparedness for singing, since he likewise has to concentrate on the piece of music to be sung—its key, colour, melody, and rhythm.

The snatched breath for Bel Canto singing is not held by the chest muscles below the larynx. The working of the *imposto* was first discovered in 1975 by B. Raymond Fink, Professor of Anesthesiology, School of Medicine, University of Washington.[3] By a tilting movement of the arytenoid cartilage—forwards, inwards, and downwards—the vocal cords are depressed and spread out horizontally in the centre of the larynx. The hyoid bone and the Adam's apple come into contact with each other. The peduncle of the epiglottis, which reaches down as far as the vocal cords, is pushed backwards in the neck, and the space within the entrance to the larynx is narrowed.

With the start of the sound being sung, e.g. 'ah!', the inner folds of the larynx, which meet firmly in the centre when the larynx is closed, are abruptly separated. Air rushes into the open larynx, momentarily from the pharyngeal cavities above, and through the windpipe from the lungs below. A 'clicking'

---

[3] *The Human Larynx*, p. 115.

sound is heard, similar to that which sounds in the mouth cavity when the tongue is separated abruptly from the hard palate.

This opening of the larynx from the *imposto* with the 'click' marks the start of the sound produced with the ventricular mechanism. When air rushes into the larynx from above and below, the ventricle of Morgagni and the adjoining sacculus are filled with air. By starting the sound from the *imposto* with the ventricular mechanism, all vocal timbres, with all their multifarious variety, can be produced.

This function of the ventricle of Morgagni at the start of the sound was hitherto unknown. I first discovered it by making the tomograms shown in Fig. 6, which revealed the inflation of the ventricle of Morgagni and the sacculus during the singing timbre 'ah!'. My findings were confirmed by Professor Gemelli. The start of the sound from the *imposto* made with the ventricular mechanism differs fundamentally from the three forms of the transient of the vocal-cord theory, which are produced by pressure from below, namely the 'firm' attack, the 'soft' or 'gentle' attack, and the 'breathed' attack.

When a singer's rib-cage is lifted and enlarged in the position of preparedness for singing, reflecting a state of aroused, alert concentration, one might expect that he has taken a deep breath; but in fact he has taken a short snap-breath, in which only a little air enters the lungs. This phenomenon has been confirmed by respiratory tests carried out in 1978 on myself and other singers by the ENT surgeon Nigel Edwards, FRCS, at the University of London Institute of Laryngology and Otology (see Appendix). The results are shown in the accompanying table.

When the chest is lifted and expanded on the rest (see Example 1 below) and the snap-breath taken, the bronchi are distended and lengthened. The pressure within the bronchi is higher than atmospheric pressure, yet much lower than when taking in the amount of air inhaled for a deep breath.

One of the features of the complex adjustments in response to being startled, the lifting of the chest, was also observed

| Subject | Breath | Volume of air (litres) | |
		Test I	Test II
Baritone	Maximum inspiration, vital capacity	6.6	7.0
	Deep breath	2.2	3.1/2.9
	Singing breath (gasp)	1.0	1.1/1.4
Soprano	Maximum inspiration, vital capacity	2.6	2.8
	Deep breath	0.88	0.99/1.03
	Singing breath (gasp)	0.44	0.62/0.22/0.4

in 1938 by Robert Curry and Douglas Guthrie, who called it 'modified breathing' or 'rib reserve'.[4] 'Rib reserve', obviously, is the position of the chest for taking a shallow breath, the gasp. Their findings were subsequently endorsed by Richard Luchsinger in *Stimmphysiologie and Stimmbildung*.[5]

In the state of concentrated preparedness for singing, the diaphragm sinks, and the contents of the abdomen are compressed. During singing, air escapes, the abdomen resumes its earlier position, and the diaphragm rises in order that the air pressure in the lungs should remain constant. Singers are inclined to support this reflex movement by contracting the abdominal muscles. The diaphragm is thereby forced too far upwards, and the volume within the lungs diminishes, making the singer feel that he has insufficient air to continue singing. This condition can be alleviated only by raising the rib-cage so that the pleurae exert a 'sucking' effect on the lungs, thus reducing the air pressure.

Celebrated singers and teachers of the nineteenth century pointed to the special breath-control required for the start of the sound in Bel Canto, stating that when singing one should feel 'as if one were taking in more air' or 'as if one were drinking a glass of wine', — cf. Francesco Lamperti, in

[4] 'The Mechanism of Breathing for Voice', *Archiv für Sprach- und Stimmphysiologie und Sprach- und Stimmheilkunde*, 2/1 (1938), 227–36.
[5] Vienna, 1951, p. 12.

his *Guida teorico-pratica-elementare per lo studio del canto*.[6]
This intuitively correct feeling has also been referred to by
Donald F. Proctor, well known as the author of *Breathing,
Speech, and Song*.[7] In his earlier book *The Physiological
Basis of Voice Training*, he quotes his Italian singing teacher
of long standing, who used to tell him that, when singing,
one should have a sensation of constantly inspiring. Evidently
his teacher was familiar with the mechanism of Bel Canto.
Proctor, however, was unable to acquire this teaching
himself, since he did not understand the specific breath-
control of the ventricular mechanism.

The state of concentrated preparedness that the singer
should adopt for the entry of a Bel Canto phrase is described
in musical notation in the exercises handed down by Busti
as preliminaries for the main Bel Canto exercises. It is
interesting to note the emphasis obtained by syncopation:
the rests are placed on the beat, the notes off the beat.

Example 1: a scale[8]

1. On the first beat of the bar, a snatched breath is taken
   and the larynx closes by the *imposto*.
2. On the second beat of the bar, the larynx opens and 'ah'
   is exclaimed.
3. In the rest on the third beat of the bar, the larynx closes.
4. On the fourth beat of the bar, an 'ah' is exclaimed with
   greater intensity on the higher note.

[6] Milan and Naples, 1865; trans. J. C. Griffith as *A Treatise on the Art
of Singing* (Milan, 1877 [1875?]).
[7] Vienna and New York, 1959.

[8] In this and all subsequent examples the bass clef is retained, following
the originals of Busti and Nava. Pupils should transpose the exercises
according to their own vocal ranges.

6 · Fundamental Principles of Bel Canto

(a) Basic exercises for vocal timbres

In the case of every instrument, the start of the sound is known as its 'transient'. In Busti's vocal exercises, the larynx must already be closed before the transient, at the beginning of the rest preceding it. During this rest the singer has to prepare himself, not only for the start of the first note, but also for the key and melody to be sung; and, most particularly, he must orientate himself, in the manner already described, for the timbre that he will use. On the second crotchet of the bar he sings the first note: the larynx opens, closing again on the third beat in order to produce the second note on the final crotchet. The singer must become familiar with the sensations that he experiences by practising these exercises from the *imposto* with the ventricular mechanism.

After the first note, sound production for the subsequent exercises continues by means of variation of pressure within the larynx. This is achieved by a valvular closing and opening of the larynx using the 'click', which the singer feels as a compression and relaxation of its viscous inner lining. Through this variation of air pressure — effected from above from the pharynx and from below from the windpipe — the larynx is provided with the exact amount of air that the singer requires for the phrase, and for the timbre that he intends to use.

Correct functioning of the ventricular mechanism is dependent on the pressure of the air in the spaces below the larynx remaining constant. This occurs as a reflex which follows the alteration of laryngeal pressure. When air is expelled from the lungs, the volume of the latter diminishes;

47

the diaphragm then rises, and the pulmonary pressure thus remains constant. But if the singer attempts to hold down the diaphragm while singing, the pressure in the air-spaces is reduced. In order to raise the pressure for voice-production, he will then compress the rib-cage involuntarily; the pressure in the lungs will increase, and he will feel ready to continue singing. In doing this, however—and it becomes plainly audible—the singer will force his tone. This is not only a strain, but also dangerous, since the involuntary forcing-out of air from the chest cavity and coronary vessels produces a higher pressure, and the return of venous blood is impeded. The face reddens, and the arteries in the neck swell visibly.

The basic elements of the ventricular mechanism, which are necessary to produce and vary voice timbres, should first be practised in the following exercise:

Example 2

The singer should not take a breath in every rest, but only as necessary. The range can be extended to an octave:

Example 3

These two exercises prescribed by Busti are fundamental for practising the use of the ventricular mechanism and the necessary breath-control. As already noted, the classical Bel Canto school left behind no instructions for practising respiration. The singer was simply told that he should adapt his emission of air to the melody that he was to sing. The singer must realize that much concentration and patience is required in order to acquire skill in using the ventricular mechanism. A similar state of total readiness for attack and production is demanded from him as is demanded from the instrumentalist. Having achieved this, he will quickly make further progress in playing his instrument.

The basic exercises for the use of the ventricular mechanism, the *vocalizzi*, must be practised in each range of vocal colour. 'Ah' is physiologically nearest to the adjustment made by the larynx in quiet production. Because of this, the singer may find difficulty in producing a crisp, sonorous 'ah'; an over-relaxed condition of the larynx results in a colourless tone. In order to produce a resonant 'ah', all parts of the larynx must be tautened. It is therefore recommended that the 'ah' be preceded by an 'ee', which will brighten the tone. It is best, moreover, to retain the bright harmonic of the 'ee' throughout when enunciating the 'ah'. When practising, the 'ah' exercise should first be sung on 'ee'.

As the sound changes from 'ah' to 'ee', the diameter of the larynx gradually narrows. The singer usually experiences this as a contraction. He need not be afraid of harming his instrument in this way. Like the mouth, the larynx resembles an elastic tube, and the well-known advice given by teachers to students to 'relax your throat' inevitably results in a voice-production lacking in sonority.

In addition to the bright timbres from 'ah' through 'é' (as in 'may') to 'ee', the singer has at his disposal darker timbres, from 'ah' through 'oh' to 'oo' and the French 'u'. These require a lowering of the larynx in the neck, effected through movements of the longitudinal muscles, which the singer feels as a downward stretching of the larynx. These darker timbres are much more difficult to produce than the bright ones. The singer must take care that the change from 'oh' to 'oo' really takes place in the larynx, and that he does not produce the sound with his lips, as many singers are easily inclined to do. Lip movements should be used only to articulate speech elements. The dark timbres like 'oh' and 'oo' can be produced only by the larynx in its low position. The lowering of the larynx must be achieved my means of the muscular loops that attach it above to the skull and below to the breastbone. If instead the larynx is pressed down from

above by the root of the tongue, the full dark timbre cannot
be produced.

(b) Development of resonances

In order to open the pharynx beyond its normal position, as
is necessary for singing, the singer should imagine gripping
a soap-bubble as if it were solid. First the jaw joint must be
separated in the manner described on p. 35–6. The singer then
imagines that he is pushing the soap bubble backwards and
downwards with the pharyngeal muscles. The pharynx will
then gradually be opened up as far down as the entrance to
the food-pipe. This requires a certain vigour, since the larynx
must be displaced forwards in the neck. The singer can
practise this opening of the lower pharynx by singing the two
basic exercises (Examples 1 and 2) on 'ah' and 'ee'. If he does
this correctly, he will learn to vary the dimension of the
pharynx and thus alter the resonances.

To achieve full use of the *imposto* mechanism, all the
resonators in the upper part of the head must be brought into
play, in order to develop 'head resonance'. The high
harmonics of the *imposto* mechanism not only give to all
the vocal registers the beauty and brilliance of Bel Canto;
they also ensure that the voice will sound in tune to a distant
listener (without adequate brilliance, a distant voice will
often sound flat even when, heard from near by, the notes
seem correctly pitched). How far these head resonances can
be brought into play depends on the skill of the singer. He
can improve his skill by practising a particular kind of
humming. He should separate his jaws, moisten his lips, and
hum the high harmonics of the *imposto* with his lips almost
closed. He must take care that the air on both sides in the
ethmoid sinuses is vibrating, and is being directed there from
the centre of the nose. The air within the forehead will also
be felt to vibrate. These exercises are of particular importance
for the development of head resonance in tenors: their 'mi-
mi-mi' exercise is well known!

(c) Messa di voce

The *messa di voce*, the 'putting-forth' or 'flourishing' of the voice (as it was translated in the eighteenth century), is an important element of Bel Canto technique. The start of the sound, as produced by the ventricular mechanism, is extended and varied in intensity and timbre. The sound begins softly with little colour. Its intensity is then increased, with a simultaneous deepening of colour. After reaching the climax of intensity and colour, the intensity is decreased and the colour diminished until the sound returns to its original quality.

Exercises for the *messa di voce* are always prominent among Bel Canto exercises. However, no explanations for these exercises are given: the empirical Bel Canto teaching of the *messa di voce* was one of the 'secrets' of the classical Italian schools. Only through X-ray films made on myself and my pupils did an analysis of the *messa di voce* first become possible for me. These films reveal clearly the individual characteristics of the *messa di voce* when it is produced with the ventricular mechanism.

Until recently it has always been accepted—and indeed it appears quite plausible—that the crescendo of the *messa di voce* requires more breath than does the decrescendo. Surprisingly, however, measurements on myself and my pupils, taken as part of my investigations at the University of London Institute of Laryngology and Otology, show that the crescendo, when produced with the ventricular mechanism, in fact requires less air than the decrescendo. This becomes understandable if one considers that when one narrows the aperture in the nozzle of a garden hose, it sends a thinner jet of water a greater distance than when the nozzle is fully open. I also showed these tests of air emission in Paris at IRCAM in a demonstration entitled 'Une nouvelle approche de la recherche musicale', in 1976. They were confirmed by Professor Jacques de Lattre, and also by Professor Arend Bouhuys who was in Paris at that time.

The *messa di voce* from the *imposto* mechanism is most effectively sung through a gradual closure of the organ of smell, which causes a simultaneous closure of the larynx, the *imposto*. During the *messa di voce* the nasal cavity and its adjacent areas are enlarged and function as resonators. When the crescendo has reached its greatest intensity and colour, their size decreases gradually as the process reverses, until their resonance dies completely away.

To practise the *messa di voce* with the ventricular mechanism requires considerable skill. As a preparatory exercise Nava recommends the *vibrazione*:

Example 4

This exercise introduces the practice of monotones linked together in legato. Example 4(*a*) begins loudly and fully coloured, at the climax of the *messa di voce*. Each successive note is sung with decreasing intensity and colour, until the sound finally dies away. In Example 4 (*b*), the first note begins softly; each successive note is increased in intensity and colour, building up to a full forte.

The *vibrazione* is a basic element in musical phrasing, used for accentuating or syncopating single notes as well as for articulating musical phrases, just as the clauses of a sentence are articulated by commas. When the singer has mastered these exercises, he can proceed to fuse the single notes into one long one, using the vowel 'ee' from the *imposto*.

(d) Mezza voce

Mezza voce is important in Bel Canto voice-production. The term is referred to in almost every teaching manual, but without any indication of how the *mezza voce* should be produced. It is generally thought that *mezza voce* denotes 'singing softly'. But it can also be sung loudly, as Caruso, for example, demonstrated in his recording of 'Una furtiva lagrima'.

The essence of *mezza voce* consists in the art of producing a very clear 'oo' from the larynx, without any movement of the lips. To achieve this, the larynx must descend markedly; the lower pharynx will simultaneously expand. While the timbres of 'ah' and 'ee' need to be sung with the body in its normal balance, for the *mezza voce* timbre 'oo' the singer must raise his centre of gravity, like a swimmer preparing to dive into the water. This change of balance is often wrongly called 'support'. Singers mistake it for drawing in the epigastrum or abdominal wall—which, however, has no effect on the body's centre of gravity, nor any influence on sound-production. The misleading concept of 'support' was unknown to the Bel Canto school.

As the production of the timbre 'oo' is lacking in high harmonics, it will frequently sound flat in pitch to the audience. This was demonstrated in a lecture given in London to the Acoustic Section of the Physical Society by the Dutch physicist van der Pol. Using an oscillator, he produced an 'oo' of moderately loud intensity, and then increased it to a forte. To the listeners, including myself, it sounded as if the pitch had dropped by two whole tones. While this 'oo' continued to sound, an 'ee', with its much higher harmonics, was produced by a second oscillator placed next to it. To the astonishment of the audience—including myself—this synthesis of 'oo' and 'ee' sounded at the original pitch, i.e. no longer flat, as it had been before the 'ee' was added. The pitch of this synthetic 'oo/ee' remained unaltered when it was varied from forte to piano.

In order that the *mezza voce* timbre should sound in tune, the singer must add some high harmonics, such as 'ee', to his *mezza voce* quality. This technique can be practised in the exercises that follow. The timbre is first sung on 'oo', (Example 5(a)), then repeated with an added 'ee', giving a French 'u' (as in 'une') (Example 5(b)). By blending 'oo' and 'ee' in this way, the correct *mezza voce* quality can be produced at the correct pitch.

Example 5

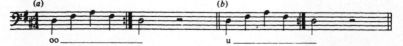

oo _____   u _____

When practising songs and arias without words, using timbres only — as singers frequently do — *mezza voce* passages should be sung with the timbre of the French 'u'.

(e) Legato

When the singer is able to produce all varieties of timbre, he must learn to play his Bel Canto instrument, beginning with the legato technique.

Every singer has a certain note in the lower middle register of his voice which he can produce without making any particular physical adjustment. This is his basic note. He can sing upwards from this note to a compass of a tenth. This is his normal register; within it, his voice will tend to rise and fall in accordance with the intensity of the emotion to be expressed. When the notes are linked together, this is known in Bel Canto terminology as 'legato'. The singer may link together not only the consecutive notes of a scale, but also notes separated by wider intervals.

In the first edition of Grove's *Dictionary of Music* an informative example is given of how Jenny Lind used to practise legato singing.[1] She began with ascending and descending intervals, linking the notes together with audible slurs, with a gliding effect between each two notes. Then she accelerated her singing of these slurred intervals, until her voice would 'shoot from note to note with lightning-like rapidity'. At such a speed the slurs would no longer be audible. This art of binding notes is a unique feature of the human voice.

Busti's first exercise for legato singing, linking one note with the next, is a scale from the keynote up to the octave and down again. According to Busti the gliding between notes should be carried out as follows:

[1] *A Dictionary of Music and Musicians* (London, 1879–89), s.v. 'Solfeggio'.

Example 6

The ascent to the octave is marked by a crescendo, indicating an increase in intensity. In the descent, each phrase is marked by both a crescendo and a diminuendo. The decrescendo marked below the stave denotes a decrease in dynamic level, while the crescendo above the stave indicates an increase in the upper harmonics on each note. This double marking is fundamental to Bel Canto legato singing.

When singing upwards, the singer should carry the phrase forward, retaining the resonance of the lower notes in the higher ones. When singing downwards, he should not relax tension completely, even though the dynamic level falls, but should retain throughout the brightness of the upper notes.

In Busti's next exercise each note is repeated, using the *vibrazione* technique as described by Nava.

Example 7

Finally the whole scale should be sung in one breath. This produces a wave-like motion, which forms the basis of the interpretation of legato singing.

Example 8

When singing the ascending exercises the singer should imagine himself to be climbing a flight of stairs. When he reaches the top he should turn round, as if on a landing, lift his centre of gravity, and sing the descending scale as if he were going down.

The same linking technique should be used for all the intervals, ensuring that the wave-like movement occurs throughout. The following exercise is intended for this purpose:

Example 9

The above can be supplemented by the following exercise, in which arpeggios and triads are sung at varying tempos:

Example 10

In the Bel Canto school a special technique, which became known as 'tessitura singing', was developed to assist the singer learning to shape musical phrases. In this technique, every note has to be given its appropriate musical value within the phrase. Before beginning the phrase, the singer must assess it musically as a whole—where it begins, how it is shaped, and where it leads to. Each phrase must be considered as one entity, not as a succession of single notes, just as we read a word as a whole, and not as the single letters of which it consists.

When a phrase, either ascending or descending, is correctly sung, the singer experiences a wave-like movement of the abdominal wall. This is due to a contraction of three segments of the rectus abdominis muscle, the outer layer of this wall. When one starts on a low note and sings an ascending phrase, this movement starts in the groin; on higher notes it travels upwards as far as the sternum. When one sings a descending phrase the reverse happens. However, these movements do not affect the deeper internal layer of the abdominal wall.

The centre of gravity of the body is at its lowest in a state of repose, approximately in the middle of the hip-girdle. It remains unchanged during an ascending phrase. But during a descending phrase the centre of gravity moves upwards. This change is usually referred to as 'support', and wrongly explained as a contraction of the abdominal wall (see p. 49).

When singing an ascending phrase with rising intensity, the singer will feel a gradual widening of his resonances in the naso-pharynx and the pharynx. The significance of the opening of these resonators was pointed out by Francesco Lamperti, the famous singing teacher of the nineteenth century, in his manual *A Treatise on the Art of Singing*.[2] He stated that the opening of these resonances gives the singer the feeling that he is continuing to inspire while singing.

(f) Mixed voice (voce mista)

Musical instruments lack the expressive capacity of the human voice, but they have a greater compass than untrained singers, whose natural compass is restricted to the tenth of

[2] See ch. 5 n. 6.

the middle register (see p. 54). If a singer endeavours to sing upwards beyond the middle register, the voice loses quality and changes into a thin falsetto. In sopranos and tenors this 'break' occurs on F, in contraltos, baritones, and basses a few notes lower. However, the Bel Canto technique provides an ingenious method of extending the singer's range, while at the same time preserving vocal quality. This technique is known as 'mixed voice'.

The singer may practise mixed voice in the following exercise. He should first sing an octave arpeggio upwards on the vowel 'ah'. On the octave he makes a decrescendo, and relaxes his *imposto* and laryngeal mechanisms. Air is felt to be floating in the nasal resonators and the pharynx. The octave is now repeated, accentuated and with bright harmonics added. At the same time the centre of gravity of the body is shifted upwards. In this position the descending arpeggio is sung.

Example 11

After the singer has mastered mixed voice-production in the middle register, he should gradually extend the range of arpeggios upwards by semitones, accentuating the higher notes by adding upper harmonics. In this way he can extend his range without his voice going into falsetto. The upper registers of mixed voice are extremely effective, but lack the many variable timbres that can be produced only in the middle register. Mixed voice-production is used especially for singing *Lieder* and oratorio.

(g) Chest voice (voce di petto)

When one sings downwards from the middle register, a change in vocal quality takes place, comparable to that which occurs in the upper register. This is known as 'chest voice'. The 'break' has an ugly sound, and in order to avoid it the Bel Canto school adopted yet another ingenious technique. The singer sings five consecutive descending notes, as in the first half of Example 12, using 'ee' quality, beginning high enough to ensure that the lowest note still remains within the middle register. He then repeats the phrase, starting on successive descending semitones. On one of these notes the 'break' will take place. It can be avoided if, on the note immediately preceding the 'break', the body's centre of gravity is raised, and the high harmonics of the 'ee' are accentuated; the descending phrase is continued now on 'ah', but emphasis is still given to the high harmonics. In this way the voice will acquire a beautiful, dark timbre, the so-called chest quality.

Example 12

When one is using chest quality, the larynx sinks down into a lower position and the lower neck expands. The centre of gravity is lifted, and strong vibrations can be felt in the upper chest. The same five notes can now be sung ascending in the chest quality. To achieve the full beauty of this timbre, the high harmonics must always remain predominant.

This extension of the vocal range upwards and downwards by the use of mixed voice and chest voice will enable the singer to vie with instrumentalists on equal terms.

7 · Mastery of Bel Canto Technique

A singer will acquire the complete musical accomplishment afforded by Bel Canto voice-production only when he has achieved control of his entire vocal compass—not only of the middle register, but also of its extension upwards by means of *voce mista* and downwards by means of *voce di petto*.

The singer must always check that he is using his instrument correctly. When he is singing downwards, the centre of gravity of his body must be lifted. He must hold his head correctly, so that an imaginary line can be drawn horizontally from the middle of the ears to the lower bones of the eye-sockets. The central point of this line between the ears is the focus of the resonators of the upper pharynx, the mouth, and the lower pharynx. To acquire control of this technique, the singer should concentrate on this central point and imagine that he is about to sing. This will bring about a contraction of the muscles of the inner ear, the stapedius and of tensor tympani, called the 'acoustic reflex', through which the singer will experience a ringing in the ears. He will then have found the optimum point from which he can control his whole vocal production. This procedure has been tested, and the theory confirmed, by experiments on me at the Institute of Physiology at the University of Münster.[1]

---

[1] See Ernest G. Weaver and Lawrence Merle, *Physiological Acoustics* (Princeton, 1954), p. 180.

61

8 · Coloratura

At the end of the seventeenth century, the Bel Canto school reached its zenith with the development of coloratura singing in the style of the Neapolitan school of Alessandro Scarlatti. The exercises for coloratura were known as *gorgheggi*. They depended on a special vocal mechanism discovered by the Bel Canto maestri, derived from the involuntary 'trembling' of the voice which can be heard in the elderly. This 'trembling' production was developed into the new coloratura technique, enabling the highest register to be sung without falling into falsetto and without singing legato. Coloratura technique can be acquired by any type of voice, male or female, high or low. Its purpose is to beautify and embellish the melodic line.

The classical nineteenth-century exercise for practising coloratura is known as the 'preparation for the trill'.

Example 13

This exercise is best begun in the middle register and later extended to other pitches. The first bar is sung legato; the second, the group of eight semiquavers, is sung without legato; the whole should be practised slowly at first, then with increasing speed. The breath 'stands still'. The larynx is tensed, and oscillates upwards and downwards between the two notes, thus producing a trill. Any attempt to produce the single notes deliberately will sound wrong.

Many singers have a natural facility for singing trills. Most, however, get bogged down in the preliminary exercises

through attempting to control their production of single
notes. The trill is finally achieved when the oscillation of
the larynx has reached a high rapidity and the breath is held
automatically, as in the warbling of a bird.

The trill can be made still more expressive by the addition
of crescendos and diminuendos. The exercises for coloratura
and the trill are sung from the *imposto*, thereby making best
use of the high harmonics and head resonances.

The exercises for practising coloratura in Bernard Lütgen's
Die Kunst der Kehlfertigkeit[1] are excellent, combining Bel
Canto voice-production with coloratura.

Example 14

Staccato is another important component of coloratura
technique. For this, the larynx is adjusted and alerted to the
vowel 'ai' (as in 'main'), and the closure at the *imposto*
tautened like a drumhead (see p. 38):

Example 15

performed

[1] New York, 1902; English edn., *Vocalises* (London, 1950).

The notes in Staccato exercises must be started from the *imposto*. With each note, the vocal production in the larynx causes a reaction in the area of the diaphragm, the movements of which can be clearly felt. During staccato singing, the breath 'stands still'. The jaw joint is separated and the jaws are kept parallel.

There are various ornaments in coloratura singing, which function as embellishments for arias and cadenzas. It is left to the artistic judgement and ingenuity of the singer to make use of them in accordance with the style of the music. One is the acciaccatura, which is practised on dotted notes. The singer feels the movement from the acciaccatura to the main note as a downward movement in the larynx. Finally the short notes are sung with increasing smoothness and rapidity.

Example 16

Fast appoggiaturas are produced by the same mechanism that is employed for the start of the first note of a group of semi-quavers, as shown in Example 13 (p. 63). They are sung softly, but with sufficient precision to facilitate the singing of the next note. Slow appoggiaturas should be sung legato. The turn should be started from the *imposto* and sung without legato:

Example 17

Scale volate are a particular form of coloratura. Starting from the *imposto*, each note is sung separately, without legato, with a slight accent:

Example 18

In the above exercise the first note of each phrase is sung in normal voice-production and ended with a *vibrazione* which is then broken off, just as a comma interrupts a sentence. This allows the singer time to prepare for the change to coloratura mechanism on the following quavers, which are sung without legato.

9 · Articulation

Once the singer has mastered his Bel Canto instrument, he has to learn to superimpose articulated vowels on the vocal timbres. The ability to combine speech elements and timbres without inferfering with the melodic line requires special skill.

There is a significant difference between the voice-production necessary for spoken words and that required for vocal timbres. Whereas speech is an amalgamation of vowels and consonants, spoken vowels are copies of vocal timbres, and are formed by the tongue, by the lips, and within the mouth cavity. In singing, articulated vowels are combined with the timbres emanating from the larynx. From this synthesis of articulated vowels and vocal timbres the singer must select the appropriate tonal colours for the music that is to be sung.

Consonants present many difficulties for the singer. Though some are 'voiced' at definite pitches, they are all to be thought of as acoustical noises, while spoken vowels are musical sounds, comprising a fundamental frequency and a series of regularly recurring harmonics. Each of these harmonics stands in a particular relationship to the fundamental. Consonants, however, do not provide a regular spectrum of harmonics and are in no way related to a fundamental. They are not sung, but have to be articulated vigorously. Sluggish and imprecise articulation of consonants distorts the rhythm and precision of a song.

Consonants preceding a syllable should be articulated before the note. Vowels should be sung on the first note itself. If a syllable begins with two or more consonants, as in 'spring', for example, these must be articulated clearly before the note. If a syllable ends with a consonant, and the next syllable or word begins with one, as in 'if that spring', then both consonants are linked together and articulated before the new syllable or word is sung.

Composers and teachers of Bel Canto always stressed the importance of singing with precise articulation. Scarlatti and Porpora composed songs without words, known as 'solfeggi', sung to the solmization syllables 'doh–ray–me–fah–soh–lah–te'. Here 'doh' serves as the tonic for each key, the following syllables representing the ascending notes of each scale. In solfeggi the singer learns to combine vocal timbres with articulated vowels and consonants. A solfeggio may modulate into a different key, for instance from C major to A minor. The singer now regards the new tonic as his 'doh', singing the following notes as 'ray–me–fah', etc. But he must ensure that all the notes of the new scale assume a minor colour of sound. From the key, rhythm, and tempo of the solfeggio, the singer must decide on the vocal timbre required, and then adjust his larynx accordingly. It is suggested that the singer places his index finger between his teeth, allowing his jaws to open, and then whispers the solfeggio. In this way he can locate exactly where the consonants and vowels are produced.

10 · Voice Types and Vocal Timbres

Today, most singers adopt a single vocal timbre, e.g. light soprano, lyric soprano, or dramatic baritone. The Bel Canto schools, however, trained their singers to sing in all vocal timbres. Thus Caruso was able to sing light as well as dramatic roles, an ability required, for example, in the different arias of the Duke in *Rigoletto*. Lilli Lehmann could sing all three female parts in *The Tales of Hoffmann* in one performance: Olympia in light quality, Antonia in lyric quality, and Giulietta in dramatic quality. Neither Caruso nor Lilli Lehmann left any explanation as to how they were able to produce these quite different vocal colours.

With the help of the Bel Canto technique, any singer can change the type of his voice. I myself sang all three female parts in *The Tales of Hoffmann* on numerous occasions. I first rehearsed the parts individually with appropriate gestures and stage movements: Olympia as a young girl, Antonia as a mature woman, Giulietta as a matron. It was only later, during the course of my research, that I discovered how these three types of voice can be produced. They result from three different configurations of the oesophagus, which are caused by the reflex action of swallowing when taking liquid or solid food: in front, by the lips, as in 'b'; in the middle, by placing the tongue against the hard palate, as in 'd'; and at the back, by the tongue against the soft palate, as in 'g'. By this means, three successive levels in the neck are inflated. Simultaneously, resonators in three sections of the chest react: the upper chest with 'b', both sides of the chest below the shoulders with 'd', and the lower area of the back with 'g'. Within the limits of his vocal equipment, the singer can adjust his production to 'b', 'd', or 'g', and sing

69

correspondingly in light, lyric, or dramatic quality. I discovered this through experiments carried out as part of my research at Chelsea Polytechnic, the London Ear, Nose, and Throat Hospital, and the Department of Phonetics, University College, London.[1]

[1] See Appendix. These findings are published in D. B. Fry and Lucie Manén, *A Basis for the Acoustical Study of Singing* (London, 1957), reprinted from *Journal of the Acoustical Society of America*, 29/6 (1957), 690-2.

Appendix: Summary of Research

The author carried out research in conjunction with the following specialists and institutions, to whom she wishes to express her gratitude:

1945–50   Dr G. McLaren, Department of Radiology, St Thomas's Hospital, London (pharynx and diaphragm).

1950–76   Drs G. M. Ardran and F. H. Kemp, Nuffield Institute for Medical Research, University of Oxford (cineradiology of larynx during singing).

1950   Professor D. B. Fry, Department of Phonetics, University College, London (voice character and analysis of vowels).

1951–5   (through Gesellschaft zur Förderung der Klangforschung, e.V., Cologne): Professor Dr Otto Kuhn and his assistant Jobst Schulze, Institute of Zoology, University of Cologne (hearing in mammals); Professor Dr K. Schneider, Institute of Physiology, University of Cologne (measurements of breathing); Dr Fritz Enkel, Technical Laboratory, West-deutscher Rundfunk, Cologne (acoustics of the voice; construction of tone-synthesizer); Professor Dr Jobst Fricke, Department of Musical Acoustics, Institute of Musicology, University of Cologne; Professor Werner Meyer-Eppler, Institute of Phonetics, University of Bonn (experiments on harmonics); Professor U. Ebbcke (larynx/trigeminal reflex); Professor E. Lerche, Institute of Physiology, University of Münster (experiments on acoustical reflex); Professor Dr V. Aschoff and his assistant Dr P. Riedel, Technische Hochschule, Aachen (experiments on pitch and volume of sound); Laboratory of Siemens & Halske AG, Berlin (physical measurements; X-rays of laryngeal function).

1978   Dr Paul Habert, Laboratory of Siemens & Halske AG, Erlangen (ultra-sound investigation, functioning of larynx); Mr N. Edwards, FRCS, and Dr M. Lunt (St Bartholomew's Hospital), Institute of Laryngology and Otology, University of London.

1979   Dr Giovanni Cavagna, Professor of Physiology, University of Milan; Padre Professor A. Gemelli, OFM, Laboratorio di Psicologia sperimentale, Università del Sacro Cuore, Milan (voice-production for singing);

1980   IRCAM (Institut de Recherche et Coordination Acoustique/Musique), Centre Georges Pompidou, Paris.

1983–4   Imperial College, London (air-flow experiments).

1984–6   Professor A. J. Fourcin (1984), Professor D. M. Howard (1986), Department of Phonetics, University College, London (formants and the ventricular mechanism).

Other authorities consulted

1959   Professor B. N. Kellogg, Department of Psychology, Florida State University, Tallahassee, Florida, USA (correspondence about hearing of dolphins).

1971   Professor R. A. Suthers, Indiana University, Bloomington, Indiana, USA.

1974   Dr N. V. Franssen, Philips Research Laboratory, Eindhoven (acoustics); Dr med. Reijsenbach, Eindhoven (ENT specialist).

1978   Professor D. Damstè, University of Utrecht (zoology; dolphins).

1976   Professor Jacques de Lattre, head of Department of Human Psychology, Sorbonne, Paris.

1976–9   Professor Arend Bouhuys, Yale University, New Haven, Connecticut, USA.

Bibliography

Ardran, G. M., Kemp, F. H., and Manén, Lucie, 'Closure of the Larynx', *British Journal of Radiology*, 26 (1953), 497-509.

Bennati, Francesco, 'Du mécanisme de la voix humaine pendant le chant', *mémoire* read to the Académie Royale des Sciences, Paris, on 25 Jan. 1830; revised version printed in *Recherches sur le mécanisme de la voix humaine* (Paris, 1832), reprinted in *Études physiologiques et pathologiques sur les organes de la voix humaine* (Paris, 1833).

Bouhuys, Arend, *Breathing: Physiology, Environment and Lung Disease* (New York, 1971, revised and enlarged, 1974).

—— Mead, J., and Proctor, D. F., 'Kinetic Aspects of Singing', *Journal of Applied Physiology*, 21 (1966), 483-96.

—— —— —— 'Mechanisms generating Subglottic Pressure', *Annals of the New York Academy of Sciences*, 155 (1968), 177-81.

—— —— —— Stevens, K. N., 'Pressure-flow Events during Singing', *Annals of the New York Academy of Sciences*, 155 (1968), 165-76.

Busti, Alessandro, *Studio di canto: Metodi classici del Conservatorio Reale di Napoli* (Naples, 1865, based on his earlier *Didascalica di canto . . .*).

Curry, Robert, *The Mechanism of the Human Voice* (London, 1940).

—— Guthrie, Douglas, 'The Mechanism of Breathing for Voice', *Archiv für Sprach- und Stimmphysiologie und Sprach- und Stimmheilkunde*, 2/1 (1938), 227-36.

Ferrein, Antoine, 'De la formation de la voix de l'homme', *Mémoires de l'Académie Royale des Sciences* (Paris, 1741), 409-32.

Fink, B. Raymond, *The Human Larynx: A Functional Study* (New York, 1975).

Fry, D. B., and Manén, Lucie, *A Basis for the Acoustical Study of Singing* (London, 1957), reprinted from *Journal of the Acoustical Society of America*, 29/6 (1957), 690-2.

Galliver, David, 'Cantare con la gorga', *Studies in Music*, 7 (1973), 10-18.

74 *Bel Canto*

Galliver, David, 'Cantare con affetto', *Studies in Music*, 8 (1974), 1-7.

—— 'The Vocal Technique of Caccini', *Poesia e musica nell'estetica del XVI e XVII secolo* (Florence, 1976), 7-11.

Garcia, Manuel Patricio Rodriguez, *Traité complet de l'art du chant* (Paris, 1840).

—— *Nouveau traité sommaire de l'art du chant* (Paris, 1856).

—— *Hints on Singing* (London, 1894).

Garcia, Manuel Vicente del Popolo, *Exercises and Method for Singing* (London, 1824).

Gray's Anatomy, 28th edn. (London, 1942).

Grove, George, ed., *A Dictionary of Music and Musicians* (London, 1879-89).

Husler, Frederick, and Marling, Yvonne R., *Singing: The Physical Nature of the Vocal Organ* (London, 1965).

Lamperti, Francesco, *Guida teorico-pratica-elementare per lo studio del canto* (Milan and Naples, 1865); Eng. trans., J. C. Griffith, *A Treatise on the Art of Singing* (Milan, 1877 [1875]).

Lehmann, Lilli, *Meine Gesangskunst* (Berlin, 1902); Eng. trans., R. Aldrich, *How to Sing* (New York, 1902; new, revised edition 1914).

Leonardo da Vinci, *Dell' Anatomia* A, *Quaderni: see* entry under MacCurdy, E.

Luchsinger, Richard, *Stimmphysiologie und Stimmbildung* (Vienna, 1951).

Lullies, Hans, *Physiologie der Stimme und Sprache* (Berlin, 1953).

Luschka, Hubert von, *Der Kehlkopf im Menschen* (Tübingen, 1871).

Lütgen, Bernard, *Die Kunst der Kehlfertigkeit: Studies in Velocity* (New York, 1902); Eng. edn., *Vocalises* (London, 1950).

MacCurdy, E., ed., *The Notebooks of Leonardo da Vinci* (London, 1938).

Mackinlay, M. Sterling, *Garcia the Centenarian and his Times* (Edinburgh and London, 1908).

Manén, Lucie, *The Art of Singing: a Manual of Bel Canto* (London, 1974).

Merkel, Karl Ludwig, *Der Kehlkopf* (Leipzig, 1873).

Meyer-Eppler, Werner, *Electronic Music* (Vienna and Bryn Mawr, 1955).

Nava, Gaetano, *Metodo pratico di vocalizzazione per le voci di basso o baritono* (Milan, n.d. [1876?])

—— *Method of Instruction for a Baritone voice*, ed. C. Santley (London, 1872).

Negus, Victor E., *The Mechanism of the Larynx* (London, 1929).

The New Oxford History of Music, iii: Ars Nova and the Renaissance 1300–1540, ed. Dom Anselm Hughes and Gerald Abraham (London, 1960).

Paget, Richard, *Human Speech* (London, 1930).

Proctor, Donald F., *Breathing, Speech, and Song* (Vienna and New York, 1959).

—— *The Physiological Basis of Voice Training* (n.p., n.d.).

Schipa, Tito, *Si confessa* (Genoa, 1961).

Sherrington, Charles S., *Selected Writings* (London, 1939).

Weaver, Ernest G., and Merle, Lawrence, *Physiological Acoustics* (Princeton, 1954).

Wilson, Robert McNairn, *The Hearts of Man* (London, 1918).